Celebrating WESTGATE

Snapshots, Historical Notes, Memories & Recipes from a Unique Columbus Neighborhood.

© 2013 Westgate Neighbors Association
Editors: Sandy Whitehead, Mari Ann Binder Futty, Betty Jaynes, Debbie Maddox
Design: Alan Jazak, Formation Studio
Printing: Capitol Citicom
Keepsake Edition Hardbound Binding: Beck & Orr
ISBN: 978-1-62620-805-6

INTRODUCTION

This project started out as a cookbook. In Westgate, though, it's not that big of a deal to have an unexpected outcome – to have a simple cookbook grow into a rich, multi-layered book about neighborhood memories and history. In our quirky, weirdly wonderful corner of the city, we just go with it! So, over the past year and a half or so, the book committee broadened its efforts.

The "Memories" section weaves together stories, reflections, photographs and, of course, a sprinkling of recipes from many perspectives, time periods and age groups. Some contributors are new to Westgate, while others are long-time residents with many adventures and tales to tell.

"Our Roots" uncovers more of what makes Westgate so "unexpected." It's not because the neighborhood was built on the site of Camp Chase, or even that the cemetery is still standing, carefully preserved — it's because so few people in Columbus know about it! It may be hard to imagine now, but as the neighborhood developed in the 1920s, Westgate became one of the most desirable neighborhoods in the city. Today, residents certainly aren't content with the state of West Broad Street; but we are intrigued and curious about the all-but-forgotten bustling economy that used to be here, and hopeful about the possibilities.

Currently, the population of Westgate is more than a mix of age, race and culture. The respectful coexistence of both progressive and traditional ideas, the blending of modern with historic elements, and even the variety of professions and income levels have encouraged a rainbow of people to make Westgate their home.

We're so proud to welcome you in for this very special visit through the homes, the streets, and through the years of Westgate. C'mon in!

Mari Ann Binder Futty,

President, Westgate Neighbors Association

WESTGATE
NEIGHBORS ASSOCIATION

The Westgate Neighbors Association dedicates this book to all past, present and future residents of our cherished neighborhood.

© 2013

OUR ROOTS

- 1   The First Landowners
- 1   Camp Chase
- 8   Neighborhood Development
- 16 Hilltop Library
- 17 Westgate Park
- 22 Historic Hilltop Bean Dinner

MEMORIES

- 30 Westgate Park
- 46 Businesses
- 64 Notable People
- 78 Gardens & Pets
- 94 Ghosts
- 104 Holidays, Parties & Celebrations
- 118 Homes
- 130 Life In Westgate
- 185 Acknowledgements

- 1 The First Landowners
- 1 Camp Chase
- 8 Neighborhood Development
- 16 Hilltop Library
- 17 Westgate Park
- 22 Historic Hilltop Bean Dinner

The First Landowners

Compiled by Mari Ann Binder Futty

In the early 1800s the land upon which the Westgate neighborhood was built was still part of the unsettled frontier. Lucas Sullivant, a surveyor, acquired ownership as payment for his work. His son Michael sold the land (known as Sullivant's Hill) to John G. Holloway of Kentucky, who later leased it to the federal government. Camp Chase was built upon that land.

Michael Lucas Sullivant

Camp Chase

The information for this chapter was provided by Richard Hoffman, Lois Neff, Patti Ongaro, Paul Clay, and by the U.S. National Park Service.

Compiled by John Futty

The eastern edge of what is now the Westgate neighborhood played a critical role in one of the most traumatic and transformative chapters in the nation's history as the site of Camp Chase during the Civil War.

The Union soldiers who passed through the camp included four future U.S. presidents. But Camp Chase is remembered in large part for its role as a Confederate prison where more than 2,000 prisoners died and whose final resting place is a cemetery in the neighborhood on Sullivant Avenue.

Dedicated in June 1861 as a training camp for Union recruits, the camp was named for Salmon P. Chase, former Ohio Governor and Lincoln's Secretary of the Treasury. It replaced Camp Jackson, which was located at the current site of Goodale Park.

Camp Chase was located on land leased by the federal government from John G. Holloway of Kentucky. The flat tract of hilltop land, four miles west of the Scioto River on the National Road, was known then as "The Racegrounds." The present-day

Prison #3 ca 1865. By M.M. Griswold.

boundaries of the Camp Chase land are South Hague Avenue to the east, West Broad Street to the north, Sullivant Avenue to the south and near South Westgate Avenue to the west.

Shortly after opening, the camp began accepting Confederate prisoners of war in a stockade built in the southeast corner of the site. The first 450 prisoners arrived in July 1861. By the time the war ended in 1865, more than 100,000 Union troops and 20,000 Confederate prisoners had passed through the camp.

Slavery at Camp Chase
U.S. National Park Service

Eight hundred enlisted men and officers of the Confederacy were the first prisoners brought to Camp Chase in February 1862. Among them were about 75 slaves and servants to the officers. Columbus citizens were outraged to learn that the African Americans continued to serve their masters even after internment. When protests from an Ohio legislative committee and horrified citizens reached Washington, D.C., federal officials were forced to act. After all had been released (by May of 1862), some enlisted in the Union army.

Among the troops stationed at the camp in the summer of 1861 were Major Rutherford B. Hayes and Private William McKinley. In August, Lt. Col. James A. Garfield arrived to take command of the newly formed 42nd Ohio Volunteer Infantry. Later in the war, Brigadier General Andrew Johnson paid a visit.

Camp Chase grew over the years of the war to the point that there were more people on the Hilltop than there were in the city of Columbus. There were about 22,000 Union troops and 9,000 Confederate prisoners at the camp in the fall of 1864.

Like other prison camps of its era, Camp Chase was a grim place. Southerners had to endure Ohio winters and suffered exposure in buildings that were made of green wood that shrank and allowed wind, snow and freezing rain into the barracks. Prison conditions became more overcrowded and unsanitary as the prison population grew from 300 to over 9,000. Disease claimed many lives during the winter of 1864–1865. In February 1865 alone, 499 men died during a smallpox epidemic.

Originally, prisoners who died at the camp were buried in the City Cemetery. The camp created its own cemetery on Sullivant Avenue in 1863, and the prisoners who had been buried in the city were moved to graves at Camp Chase.

By the time the camp closed in July 1865, 2,260 Confederates had died while imprisoned there.

The camp's 160 wooden structures were dismantled after the war, leaving only the two-acre cemetery, with graves marked by wooden slats and surrounded by a low fence. The cemetery quickly fell into disrepair.

Although badly neglected, the grounds drew the attention of many groups, including both Union and Confederate veterans. In the late 1880s federal funds were used to procure a 16-ton boulder, the cemetery's first monument. Carved into the boulder were the words "2,260 CONFEDERATE SOLDIERS OF THE WAR 1861–1865 BURIED IN THIS ENCLOSURE."

Then in 1893 William H. Knauss, a former Union colonel who was wounded in the battle of Fredericksburg, moved to Columbus. He learned of the Confederate cemetery on the west side of the city and discovered that the burial place was in bad condition.

The gates and gateposts had crumbled; the grounds were overrun with weeds and stray animals. Knauss arranged with Henry Briggs, owner of a farm opposite the cemetery, to have it cleaned up. In the spring, a few friends distributed some flowers about the place.

Knauss planned a small memorial service in 1895. The trees were trimmed, the gates and gateposts reset, and the brush once again cleared. Three days before the planned service, most participants backed out, fearing reprisals from friends. However, a small group of 50 did attend that first service. In 1896 and 1897 a more favorable atmosphere prevailed. Almost 1,500 people attended the 1897 service.

In 1902 a stone arch — engraved with the word "Americans" and topped by a statue of a Confederate soldier facing south — was dedicated in the cemetery. The annual memorial service was turned over that year to the local chapter of the Daughters of the Confederacy.

The wooden grave markers eventually were replaced by marble headstones, which were funded by an act of Congress in 1906. The stone wall surrounding the cemetery and the speaker's platform were constructed in 1921.

In 1995, on the 100th anniversary of the first service, the Hilltop Historical Society was asked to assume organization of the memorial services. They continue to be held each year on the second Sunday in June and are dedicated to the memory of all who were at Camp Chase, and in honor of all American soldiers who have lost their lives in military conflicts.

The federal government began renovations of the cemetery in 2009. Headstones were raised, leveled, straightened, and in some cases, replaced. In 2010, the arch and statue were repaired, and all was finished in time for the 2011 memorial service – the 150th anniversary year of the start of the Civil War.

The Camp Chase Confederate Cemetery at 2900 Sullivant Avenue is one of 33 soldiers' lots and Confederate cemeteries maintained by the National Cemetery Administration, Department of Veterans Affairs. The site is open to the public under the supervision of the Dayton National Cemetery.

The 4 Mile House was located across from the entrance to Camp Chase, where Hoge Memorial Presbyterian Church now sits. It served as officers' headquarters, and as housing for camp visitors. The 4 Mile House, so named because it was 4 miles from downtown Columbus, was torn down in 1913.

This photograph of a northeast section of Westgate was taken in 1949. West Broad Street runs across the top of the photo (east - west), and the northern portion of Binns Boulevard runs through the middle (north - south). Also pictured: portions of Crescent Drive, Olive Street, South Huron and South Roys Avenues. Photo provided by Jeff Wise and Andy Lucas.

Neighborhood Development

Compiled by John Futty

As the 1920s arrived, most of what would one day be the Westgate neighborhood was woods, fields and farmland.

The Columbus city limits ended at Hague Avenue in 1920. Houses lined Hague south of West Broad Street, but the only streets to the west were Powell and Chase avenues. There had been little development in the area since the federal government abandoned the Camp Chase site 50 years earlier. Members of a large Quaker settlement in Jefferson County had purchased more than 400 acres of Hilltop land that included the old camp site in 1872, hoping to create a new Quaker settlement. William Binns and Robert Hague, whose family names would one day be given to streets in the neighborhood, were among those who purchased land.

But residential development west of Hague didn't take off until the early 1920s when the Pavey-Johnson Realty Co. acquired land to create a "streetcar suburb." At the time, the Camp Chase streetcar route began Downtown and traveled west up Sullivant

Camp Chase Trolley

Historical marker on West Broad Street. Photo by Alan Jazak.

Avenue, then went north on South Hague to West Broad. The streetcar headed west on Broad to the Big Four railroad crossing near Wilson Road, which was in the country. West Broad also was a key transportation link as part of the National Road, the first major improved highway in the U.S., linking Maryland to Illinois. Westgate was born along West Broad about the same time the National Road was being absorbed into U.S. Rt. 40.

Many of the houses on South Hague were built between 1910 and 1920. There also are four houses on the west of side of Chase, just north of today's St. Mary Magdalene ballfields, that were built around 1915. Two houses in the 400 block of Powell also date to that era. But Franklin County auditor's office records indicate that construction of the first houses in what became a nearly decade-long building boom in Westgate began in 1923. The neighborhood, which developed west from Hague and south from Broad, is a combination of subdivisions that originally were plotted as Broadview, Broadview Extension, Camp Chase Heights, Westgate and Westgate Park.

In 1924 Pavey-Johnson Realty Co. ran large advertisements in The Columbus Evening Dispatch offering lots for sale as low as

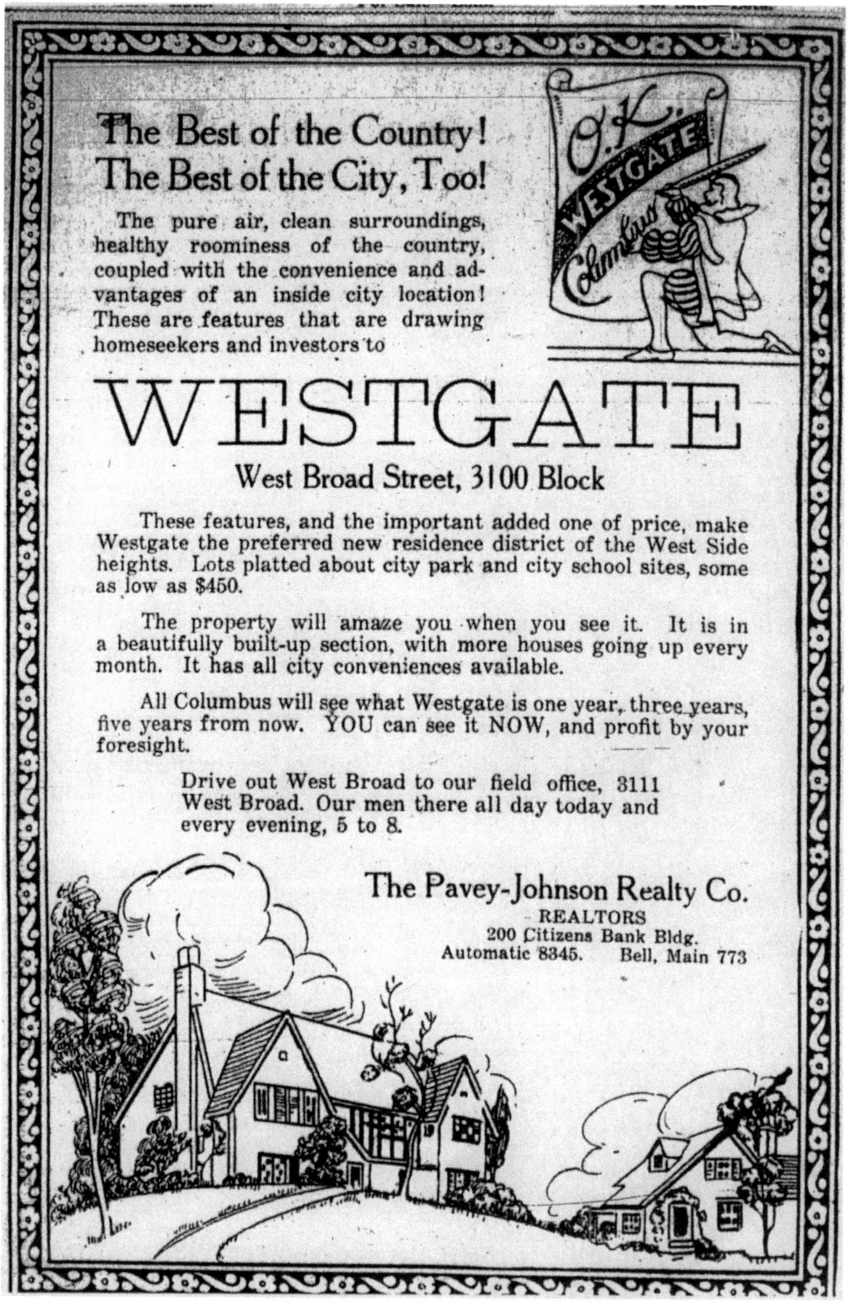

The Best of the Country! The Best of the City, Too!

The pure air, clean surroundings, healthy roominess of the country, coupled with the convenience and advantages of an inside city location! These are features that are drawing homeseekers and investors to

WESTGATE
West Broad Street, 3100 Block

These features, and the important added one of price, make Westgate the preferred new residence district of the West Side heights. Lots platted about city park and city school sites, some as low as $450.

The property will amaze you when you see it. It is in a beautifully built-up section, with more houses going up every month. It has all city conveniences available.

All Columbus will see what Westgate is one year, three years, five years from now. YOU can see it NOW, and profit by your foresight.

Drive out West Broad to our field office, 3111 West Broad. Our men there all day today and every evening, 5 to 8.

The Pavey-Johnson Realty Co.
REALTORS
200 Citizens Bank Bldg.
Automatic 8345.   Bell, Main 773

Columbus Evening Dispatch, Sunday, July 27, 1924.

$450 in "the remarkable new residential development" known as Westgate. One of the ads promised: "The pure air, clean surroundings, healthy roominess of the country, coupled with the convenience and advantages of an inside city location!" It also boasted... "All Columbus will see what Westgate is one year, three years, five years from now. YOU can see it NOW, and profit by your foresight!"

The 1924 city directory included the first mention of Binns Boulevard, with six houses listed. South Roys Avenue, Olive Street, South Westmoor Avenue and Girard (renamed Wicklow Road in 1933) each had one house.

Residential construction boomed in 1925 as South Westgate Avenue (20 houses), Crescent Drive (8 houses), South Brinker Avenue (6 houses), South Huron Avenue (3 houses) and Ellis Place (2 houses) made their first appearances in the city directory. Binns had grown to 32 houses, South Roys to 12, South Westmoor to 11, Guernsey to 10 and Olive Street to 5. Two other significant developments occurred in 1925: The Westgate Masonic Lodge opened on West Broad Street and the Columbus City Schools purchased property on Powell for a new West High School.

Construction of the Georgian Revival-style school began in 1926 and the building was dedicated in 1929. The school was designed by Howard Dwight Smith, the same architect who designed Ohio Stadium. (The new building replaced the former high school on South Central Avenue, which became Starling Middle School.)

In 1926 Palmetto Street showed up in the directory with its first 3 houses. Fremont got its first house west of Hague. That also was the first year businesses began to adopt the neighborhood name as they set up on West Broad: Westgate Electric Shop, Westgate Barbecue and Westgate Auto Company.

The 1927 city directory showed Palmetto Street with five houses and Parkside Road with two, all east of Binns. Powhatan Avenue got its first three houses that year. Demorest Road appeared in that directory with 12 addresses, even though there were no other houses west of Powhatan in the neighborhood.

South Algonquin Avenue (4 houses) and South Sylvan Avenue (3 houses) made their first appearances in the 1928 directory. Also that year the United Brethren Church was built at 61 South

These houses, 36 and 42 South Huron Avenue, were 2 of the first 3 built on South Huron in 1925.

Powell. The building has housed the Westgate United Methodist Church since 1968.

In 1929 St. Mary Magdalene's original brick building, which housed the Catholic church and school, was dedicated at 2940 Parkside Road.

The neighborhood saw modest residential growth in 1929 and 1930 as the Great Depression dawned. The devastating economic downturn stalled the neighborhood's development for much of the 1930s. For example, South Southampton Avenue got its first house in 1929, but didn't get another until 1938. Powhatan had 23 houses in 1932, and it too, didn't see any additional construction until 1938. Letchworth Avenue existed as a city street as early as 1927, but didn't get its first house until 1939.

Nowhere was the effect of the Depression more evident than in the delayed residential development around Westgate Park. In 1929 there was one house facing the park on Westgate Avenue and one on Parkside Road. No other houses were built around the park until 1937. Wicklow got its first house on the park in 1939. Demorest had no houses on the park until 1940.

There were clear indications that Columbus and Westgate were pulling out of the Great Depression in the late '30s and early '40s. Brinker went from 42 houses in 1937 to 72 in 1939. Letchworth grew from one house in 1941 to 25 in 1942.

In 1941 the Columbus District of the Methodist Church and the Riverside Charge began exploring the idea of building a church in Westgate. After first holding services in West High School, the congregation bought the triangle of land where Algonquin and Brinker meet at Wicklow across from Westgate Park in 1944. Westgate Methodist Church held its first service on the site in December 1946. The original church included a basement sanctuary, with one story of limestone walls above ground.

Westgate's residential growth slowed again after America's entry into World War II, followed by another surge after the war. South Sylvan, for instance, was stuck on 35 houses from 1942 to 1946. In 1947 it had 58. That number had grown to 81 by 1950 and 96 by 1960.

Construction of neighborhood amenities also picked up after the war. Although the city schools purchased land for Westgate

This advertisement appeared in the Columbus Evening Dispatch on Sunday, June 22, 1930 less than 8 months after the stock market crash.

Parkview United Methodist Church

Elementary School in 1923, the school wasn't built until 1952 to accommodate the children of the post-WWII baby boom. Another place of worship was added to the neighborhood with the construction of the Community Christian Church at 107 South Powell from 1948 to 1952.

Post-war growth at St. Mary Magdalene and Westgate Methodist churches led to expansion for both congregations in the 1950s. St. Mary Magdalene built Raymond Hall in 1950 as a meeting hall and rec center, but almost immediately made it part of the school. Ground was broken for a new church on South Roys in 1954 with its dedication in 1956. Westgate Methodist outgrew its basement home and raised money to complete the modified Gothic church and bell tower. The expanded building was dedicated in 1955. The church was renamed Parkview United Methodist in 1968.

Most housing construction in the neighborhood was finished by the 1960s, although the newest house was built in 2004 at the corner of Powhatan and Palmetto.

The neighborhood is distinguished by its variety of architectural styles and building materials. Westgate has homes of stone, brick and frame construction in styles ranging from Cape Cod to Dutch Colonial, from Tudor Revival to American Foursquare. The development wasn't always orderly, adding to the neighborhood's uniqueness. It isn't unusual, for instance, to find a house built in the 1920s beside one built in the 1940s.

Through it all, Westgate has remained, as promised by its earliest developers, a "remarkable" neighborhood, one of the most stable and picturesque in the city.

St. Mary Magdalene Catholic Church

Originally built to house both St. Mary Magdalene Catholic Church and school, the Parkside Road building is now used exclusively as a school building.

Hilltop Library

Submitted by Cynthia Steinke Anderson

In 1911 the Sunset Literary Club established a library on the second floor of the West Broad Elementary School, located on the NE corner of West Broad Street and North Hague Avenue. The library, operated by members and neighbors, started with 300 donated books. After a decade of collecting books, in 1921 the literary club received the private book collection of Lawrence Holmes. The books were in storage for two years before the library name changed to the Holmes Library. The library opened on the second floor of the Hilltop Branch of the Citizens Trust & Savings Bank located at South Wayne Avenue and West Broad Street For the first time, the library hired a person to be in charge of the daily operations. Hired for the position was Nannie Wilkens Currier, a widow with four small children.

The name Holmes Library changed to the Hilltop Library in 1928. Funding from the Columbus Public Library enabled the library to relocate to 21 North Hague Avenue. It opened on October 4, and remained in this building for 22 years.

March 1, 1950 the library again relocated to the corner of W. Broad and Binns Boulevard. Located at 2955 W. Broad, and on Camp Chase land, the cost of the library was $47,000 and was the first public owned library in the city.

The Hilltop Library at West Broad Street and Binns Boulevard in 1965. Today the building houses Ohio Radio Reading Services.

Opened in 1996 the present library is located near the SW corner of South Hague Avenue and Sullivant Avenue and again resides on the historic grounds of Camp Chase. Often when there are strange building issues or weird computer happenings, it is blamed on Confederate ghost soldiers.

Incorporated in the newest library are artifacts from the Columbus State Hospital. Included are ornate ceiling beams, a fireplace and iron insert, stained glass windows, walnut and mahogany Newell post and railing; plus a replica of the towers that once rested above the roof line of the hospital is now located on the roof line of the library.

Interior of the Hilltop Library at Binns Boulevard and West Broad Street during the 1960s.

Westgate Park

Submitted by Sue Laughlin

Westgate Park came into existence between April 24, 1924 and November 5, 1925, during James J. Thomas' term as mayor of Columbus. The anchor and centerpiece of the Westgate neighborhood was made possible by the generous donations (almost 50 acres) of Lydia Hussey, David Pugh et al, Mary C. Foley et al, and the Pavey-Johnson Realty Company.

In the 1930s the first Hilltop Bean Dinner took place in Westgate Park. The roots of the historic event actually go back further, to just after the Civil War. Sponsored by the Hilltop Business Association, the annual community festival is still held at the park each June.

In 1933 the first of two water towers was installed in the park. The coned tower, put into service in October of that year, can hold 1,000,000 gallons of water. The second rounded tower, installed 19 years later, was operational as of July 1952.

By 1938 the Hilltop Record was heralding the opening of the new "first class" clay tennis courts being built by the Works Progress Administration (W.P.A.). A fee of ten cents per hour was reported as a way to recoup some of the building costs. That same paper also reported minor improvements being made to the baseball diamonds that were also created by the W.P.A.

In 1939 playground equipment and a children's wading pool were in place. But the biggest improvement that year was the construction of Harder Lake (known as "the pond"), which was built by enlarging an existing natural lake on the property. The lake is included on the website www.ohiogamefishing.com for fishermen to recount their stories of "the ones that got away."

The Betty Bricker Memorial Garden was created to honor community gardener and activist Betty Bricker who worked tirelessly for Westgate and the Hilltop. Photo by Alan Jazak.

Harder Lake fountain, looking south, southeast. Photo by Alan Jazak.

For years, the pond was home to many rousing games of ice hockey and the open shelter's fireplace warmed both skaters and spectators.

The Harder Lake fountain we see today, originally designed in 1951 by architect and OSU Professor George B. Toby as a replacement for a previously deteriorated fountain, was finally installed in 1994. This would not have been possible without the tireless efforts of the community volunteers of Friends of Westgate Park (FOWP) and the Community Recreation Council of the Westgate Recreation Center.

Few people know that in 1945 there were plans for Westgate Park to have a band shell and a skating rink built. The rink was to be used for roller-skating in the warm months and for ice-skating during the winter. Although 700 Hilltop residents donated money during a fundraising campaign, there was not enough money raised to move ahead with the plans for the rink and band shell. The money was saved instead and twenty years later added to money raised through the passage of a bond issue in 1960 to build the Recreation Center we know today. The center was dedicated in 1965 and stands today as one of the busiest in the city.

Left: Mr. Griffin's 1959 Class at Westgate Elementary School.

Opposite: Curtis Goldstein's mural "The Heroes of Camp Chase" in Westgate Park.

Sports and sporting events have always been a central feature of the park. In addition to ice-skating, basketball, tennis, baseball, football and soccer, Westgate Park was once home to a series of racquetball tournaments started in 1985.

The tournaments, organized to benefit Columbus Children's Hospital, raised thousands of dollars to support the facility. In the first year more than 300 players signed up. (A woman from Cincinnati actually cut short her trip on an African safari to attend the tournament.) Players came to Westgate from at least ten states to compete. In 1986 a team match was played between

West High School, Powell Avenue

Columbus and Rochester, New York. Today, the courts are used to play racquetball and handball. Westgate is the only park in the city to have outdoor racquetball courts.

In 1985 a double elimination softball tournament was held in Columbus with the women playing at Westgate and Deshler Parks while the men played at Berliner. Also in 1985 as part of the annual Historic Hilltop Bean Dinner, a 10K run was held with its starting and ending spots in the park.

There have been recent additions to the park. In 2009 FOWP raised thousands of dollars to install a mural designed and painted by Columbus muralist and artist Curtis Goldstein. The mural depicts scenes taken from historical documents relating the story of the Civil War and the Camp Chase training facility and prisoner of war camp; it includes quotations reflecting the beliefs of Abraham Lincoln and Salmon P. Chase on the injustice of slavery. A second mural celebrating the city's 200th birthday is in the works. The central theme will be children at play in the park.

Also in 2009 FOWP and Friends of the Scioto River worked together to install a rain garden near the park's enclosed shelter house – the first of its kind in a Columbus city park. The garden includes native plants that attract birds and butterflies. The specially designed garden collects rainwater from a nearby parking lot and filters out pollutants from the runoff.

In 2010 FOWP launched the Belgian Mum Project, working with

GroLink of Oxnard, CA, the only distributor of Belgian mums in the U.S. GroLink sends hundreds of plant cuttings each year, which are planted in the research bed and tended to by volunteers. A report is then sent back to the company, outlining the growth and hardiness of the mum varieties. If a mum survives the winter, it is transferred from the research bed to a display bed. To date, the park has three display beds in addition to the research bed.

In 2011 the enclosed shelter house underwent a major renovation, including the construction of two patios.

Westgate Park is constantly evolving and yet still remains a place in our collective memory for old-fashioned fun; a place where childhood memories were created long ago, or are being forged today among a new generation of park enthusiasts.

The Historic Hilltop Bean Dinner

Submitted by Sandy Whitehead

Following the Civil War, veterans of both sides held reunions to honor their dead, reminisce and cook simple foods eaten during the war campaigns – beans, cornbread (if you were lucky) and coffee. While some dinners in southern Ohio began more than 130 years ago, The Hilltop Bean Dinner did not commence until the 1930s, and was sponsored by the group now known as the Hilltop Business Association (HBA).

The dinner became a community festival — at one point a three-day event — under the direction of the HBA. Thousands came for jitterbug dancing, greased pole and greased pig contests, beauty pageants, games, band concerts and carnival rides. Business owners offered prizes to whoever guessed the correct number of beans in glass jars displayed in their shop windows. One highlight was the hotly contested Tug-of-War between the Lions and Kiwanis Clubs at Harder Lake, which ended with the winning team dragging the losers into the water.

Prior to 1947 the beans, cooked with ham over open fires, were free. In 1947 the price of beans jumped to around 14 cents per pound – an exorbitant price – causing the dinner to be cancelled. It resumed the following year.

The Hilltoppers vs. The Ohio Village Muffins, June 2010

The present day Bean Dinner, held the fourth Saturday of June, still offers the traditional beans and cornbread, games, kiddie rides and music, but also includes an art show, food vendors, and a display of classic cars. History is an important part of the day, with members of the Hilltop Historical Society dressing in 19th century costumes and Civil War uniforms, telling stories and recounting events. At the 2010 dinner, a group of Hilltop residents played a game of baseball against the Ohio Village Muffins, a 19th century reenactment team sponsored by the Ohio Historical Society. Both teams played in authentic reproduction uniforms, and by rules in place during the 1860s. It was a "no girls allowed" affair, with fines incurred to any gentleman player caught spitting or swearing.

1931 Bean Dinner

Calico Beans

SUBMITTED BY JUNE BEARD

1 pound ground meat
2 tablespoons vinegar
1 small onion, chopped
¾ cup brown sugar
½ cup ketchup
1 teaspoon dry mustard
15 oz. can pork & beans
15 oz. can red kidney beans
15 oz. can butter beans

1. Drain water from kidney and butter beans
2. Brown ground meat and onion together
3. Drain excess grease and mix all ingredients together
4. Bake at 350 for 30-45 minutes or put in Crockpot for 1 hour

Cowboy Beans

Submitted by Sandy Whitehead

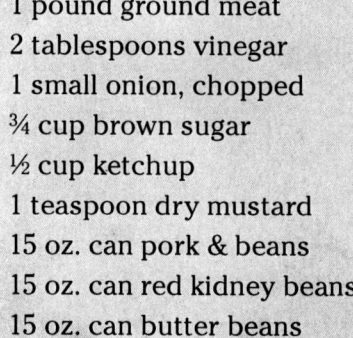

1 pound dry pinto beans
7 cups water
2 - 12 oz cans "lite" beer
1 pound smoked ham hocks
½ cup chopped onion

1-16 oz can tomatoes cut up
3 tablespoons molasses
1 teaspoon dry mustard
¼ teaspoon pepper

1. Rinse beans and combine with seven cups water. Bring to a boil.
2. Simmer for two minutes then remove from heat. Cover and let stand for one hour then drain.
3. Combine beans, beer, one-cup water, ham hocks and onion; cover and simmer for one hour, stirring occasionally.
4. Remove ham hocks, take meat from bones and chop. Discard bones.
5. Return meat to beans and add tomatoes, molasses, dry mustard and pepper.
6. Cover and simmer one more hour or until beans are tender. Stir occasionally. Add additional water or beer if needed.

My Grandmother's Cornbread

Submitted by Sean Harmon

Ingredients:

- 1 ½ cups yellow cornmeal
- ½ cup all purpose flour
- 2 tsp baking powder
- 1 tsp salt
- 3 tbsp white sugar
- 1 large egg
- 2 cups milk
- ½ cup (1 stick) unsalted butter

Grease a 10" diameter cast iron skillet with peanut oil or shortening. Place the skillet in the oven while you preheat the oven to 450F.

1. Mix all the dry ingredients together in a large mixing bowl with a fork or a whisk.
2. In a separate bowl, beat the egg and whisk in the milk.
3. Melt the stick of butter and slowly beat it into the egg and milk mixture.
4. Combine all ingredients in the large bowl and stir until just well mixed.
5. Let sit for five minutes.
6. Give the mixture a quick stir and pour it into the preheated skillet.

Reduce the oven temperature to 425F and bake the cornbread for 20-25 minutes. Remove when the top just begins to brown. Invert the skillet over a large flat plate.

This works well with soups, beans, or by itself.

Scotch Shortbread *submitted by Ric Brandel*

Cream 1 c. butter and ½ c. sugar until fluffy. Stir in 2-½ c. flour. Chill 2 to 5 hours. Divide in half, pat into 7-inch circle, and prick with fork to make pie shape or press into shortbread mold. Bake at 300 degrees for 30 minutes.

Westgate
MEMORIES

- 30 Westgate Park
- 46 Businesses
- 64 Notable People
- 78 Gardens & Pets
- 94 Ghosts
- 104 Holidays, Parties & Celebrations
- 118 Homes
- 130 Life In Westgate
- 185 Acknowledgements

Westgate Park

Looking from the park at 3336 Wicklow Road in 1951.

Lantern Parade

Submitted by Beth Loughner

During the summer months (between 1966 and 1977), every elementary school (Eakin, Binns, etc.) became a city "rec" center. The Recreation and Parks department hired two college students (one woman and one man) for each elementary school. Part of the school building (usually 2-3 rooms) was open between noon and 8:00 pm. I went to Georgian Heights Elementary. We did all kinds of crafts, organized games and even had softball teams that competed between schools.

During late July, we had the lantern parade. Each kid was given a box (old boxes from grocery stores) and we would cut out designs on each of the four sides. We would then either glue or tape colored cellophane over each cut-out. A handle was made to carry the box. Two or three candles were then glued to the inside bottom of the box. The parade was held at dusk around the pond. There were usually enough kids to totally go around the pond. We would then walk around the pond, the lanterns aglow with color and reflecting in the water. Usually, one or two kids didn't glue their candles in well or too close to the sides, and their box would catch fire. They would toss the flaming lantern into the pond. The lantern parade really was beautiful, and the highlight of my summer.

Picnics with Mother

Submitted by Joanne Horn Hylton

My earliest memories of Westgate Park date to about 1938. On Saturday nights the Horn family went grocery shopping. The A & P, which my parents patronized, was then located on the northwest corner of Chase and W. Broad. As a special treat, my brother Jerry, my sister Nancy and I were taken to play on the swings or sliding board at the park before we shopped.

On rare occasions, my mother would take us to the park for a picnic. Mother didn't drive, so we walked from our home on S. Ogden Ave. She pulled a wagon in which my sister rode along with the picnic supplies and a large cast iron skillet in which Mother fried little pig sausages and potatoes on grills near concrete tables distributed about the woods.

The only buildings in Westgate Park then were the stone shelter house, still standing; two pit-toilets, which we would only use out of desperation; and the shed, which housed maintenance equipment for the tennis courts. The tennis courts received a lot of use because they were among the few public clay courts available.

A shallow wading pool was a popular cooling off spot for children in the summer when the spray was turned on. When I became a parent, I took my children to that wading pool, so it is a part of their memories, as well.

The lake was twice as large as it is today and surrounded by large willow trees. The banks were badly eroded due to heavy use by fishermen. Children were warned that the westernmost end of the lake had quicksand, although I never put that to a test.

When the lake was constructed, the excess soil was dumped at the southern end of the park to form a large hill. The hill was a warren of rabbits and covered with wild rose shrubs, which made climbing it a challenge. In winter, sledding was equally challenging because there were many large old-growth trees at the foot of the hill that had to be avoided.

At this time, the park was more like the pasture it once was. (Doris Barnes Fledderjohann recalled when the park was the Derrer cow pasture.) The woods were marshy, and in spring violets could be picked by the handfuls.

The park experienced a series of renovations in later years. The lake was reduced in size, the sides were lined with concrete, and it was renamed Harder Lake. The soil of the hill was trucked back and used to fill in the western part of the lake. Originally, it was expected that a sunken rose garden would be created, but the area is too swampy.

Harder Lake fountain, looking north, northeast at the open shelter house. Photo by Alan Jazak.

Park Parades, Events and Contests

Submitted by Linda Barnhart Lowry

Lantern Parade – we made our lanterns at the green shelter house. Could decorate it however you wished. Then had a parade around the park and pond. What a lovely sight with all the lit lanterns.

Pet Parade – kids would bring their pets all dressed up and some were pulled in wagons and paraded around. Then a winner was chosen.

Clown Contest – kids would dress up and with their homemade clown costumes. Parade in park to see costumes and then a winner was chosen.

Casting Tournament at the pond – Park Supervisor would put big plastic rings in middle of pond. Contest was held to see who could cast their line with casting plug into rings. Winner got a prize. Many times, it was a new casting plug.

Hilltop Community Theater – held 2 productions of musicals in the park. My daughter was in the live orchestra they had. "Westside Story" was the 1st one done in the park. They did it for 2 nights. Actors, actresses, orchestra, etc., all donated their time. People came with their chairs and packed the place. They also did "Oklahoma!," which was done the following year, but it was moved up near the closed shelter house. Great turn out again. After that, it was moved to West High School, then Hillcrest Baptist Church and then Wedgewood Middle School. Eventually the live orchestra was done away with and they used taped music. I know they also did "Oliver Twist," "Finian's Rainbow" and "Bye Bye Birdie." Think they did "Finian's Rainbow" at West. Aaron Jackson (Briggs H S Music Director) was the conductor for "Music Man"; Mark Sampson (West H S Music Director) was the conductor for "Oklahoma."

Music In The Park – there was a bandstand every Sunday near the closed shelter house where there was a concert. People would bring their chairs and enjoy the music. My dad would meet my husband and I at the park and we would enjoy the music so much. Was done away with after many years.

Tennis Courts – always busy. You had to get on a waiting list, sometimes waiting one hour before you could get a court. You were limited to one hour of playing time. Remember that Judge Draper would play there a lot.

Little Green Shelter House – used to sit near where little kids playground is now (near tennis court). Always something to do there, crafts, tetherball, sports for kids, basketball court near and big playground was nearby too. Had softball, volleyball and track teams for the girls. We competed against other parks. Mary Gilliam was the Girls Park Supervisor. We always had good participation and won many championships. There was a ball diamond where the small children's park now is. That is the diamond where we practiced. Games were held at ball diamond near the field at the closed shelter house.

Aftermath of Hurricane Ike – what a sad day for the park. Many trees were lost. My husband and I rode our tandem bike through the park and took pictures of the damage. Many of the trees I watched grow are now gone.

Ice Skating At The Pond – spent after school and evenings ice skating. Remember fireplace in open shelter house had a fire going all the time to go in and warm up. Had tree stumps or picnic tables we could sit on near the fire. Had to bring our own hot chocolate or whatever else we wanted to eat. There were also concrete benches on sidewalk around pond where you could sit to put on your skates.

Westgate Pond – when I was growing up there were little "inlets" with weeping willow trees. Really not supposed to but kids would swing on end of tree limbs out over the pond. Many a time kids didn't make it back to inlet and went into the pond. Sometimes on

Early picture of Harder Lake.

purpose. I spent many hours fishing at the pond. Caught a couple of turtles. Many times, you could catch little bluegills, little catfish and tadpoles with your hands just walking around the edge of the pond.

Memories of the Hilltop Bean Dinner

The Bean Dinner went on for several days and was always busy.

Free Bean Soup – mother made me go to the park with big pan to get the bean soup for dinner. The bean soup was homemade.

Queen Contest was held on the stage in the middle of the park.

Amusement Rides all over the park on Parkside Drive. There were booths and tents with many displays. On one day there was a special rate for rides.

Tug Of War – held over pond. Groups were invited to do the tug of war.

Had a stage for entertainment, contests, etc. in the middle of park.

People would walk around and visited with each other. Always something to look at or visit with people.

Cars were parked up and down the streets — hard to find parking places at times, especially the weekend. We were lucky that we lived close enough to walk and could go home and rest and go back to different events.

Cars In The Park – in existence for 27 years and still going strong. Started in 1985 by Jim Stewart (Stewart Motor Cars). He ran the show from 1985 through 2005. Car Show started out on the Parkside Rd. side of the park. After several years was moved to Wicklow Rd. side of the park. Complaints that the weight of the cars was ruining the roots of the trees. Jim Stewart gave the car show up after many years due to health reasons; he recently passed away. A-Tech (located on Eakin Rd.) took over the show in 2006. The car show has grown every year. In 2012 there were cars parked from the open shelter house all the way down to the tennis courts. What a sight — all those antique, collector cars and talking with the people showing them. We have shown our 1965 GTO since 1987, and showed our 1967 NSU Wankel Spider convertible in 2002. We have received many trophies over the years.

Pictured in the center is Linda Barnhart Lowry helping her mother serve punch at the Christmas Tea held for Campfire Girls troop leaders in 1960.

Linda with some of her Campfire Girls troop.

Playtime, Picnics & the Ponytail Pageant

Submitted by Elizabeth Hylton

My mother would take us for a playtime and, on occasion, for picnics at Westgate Park. As we grew older, we went to the park on our own. Sometimes, we would take brown bag lunches to the picnic area at the west end of the park before heading over to the playground. We loved the big slide and the monkey bars. When the Kiddie Corral opened we enjoyed going on the merry-go-round. One time, we made it go so fast that I broke a toe while jumping on.

In the summertime, the water was turned on in the wading pool. Later a ceramic turtle which sprayed water from the top was added and children would sit on it and get wet. Eventually, the wading pool was filled with mulch and large concrete A B C letters and a steel snail that had been in the play area at Westland Shopping Center were installed.

At Easter, an Easter Egg Hunt was held in front of the enclosed shelter house. Cream filled chocolate eggs in brightly covered wrappers were hidden all over. Many children participated in that event — so many, that one might come home empty handed.

Our family looked forward to attending the Bean Dinner. We enjoyed the rides and visiting the exhibits. One year my grandmother entered me in the ponytail contest, my one and only pageant.

From time to time I would sign up for some of the activities at the Westgate Recreation Center. I took classes in cooking, sewing, arts and crafts, and gymnastics. The gymnastics teacher, Lisa Galat, had been an Olympic competitor. She also taught arts and crafts at the recreation center. After she left the center, she went on to open a cooking school in Columbus and she bought, restored and ran the Clock Restaurant in downtown Columbus.

Grilled Glazed Salmon
~ Submitted by Mari Ann and John Futty ~

The Salmon:

1. Soak thick-cut salmon filets in milk for at least an hour.
2. Pat dry. Preheat grill on highest setting.
3. Grill fish (skin-side down on pierced foil or in a basket) covered for 8-10 minutes (until nearly done), then brush with glaze and continue cooking for 3-6 more minutes until fish flakes easily.
4. Serve with remaining hot glaze.

The Glaze:

Stir the juice and zest of one lime (about ¼ cup) into 1 cup peach preserves; heat until bubbly. The amounts can be adjusted to taste.

Note: If you don't care for 'sweet' fish, grill the salmon as above, except skip the glazing and serve with dill sauce:

The Dill Sauce:

Add snipped, fresh dillweed to 1 cup sour cream or plain yogurt. Stir in 1-2 TBSP of fresh lime juice to taste.

Serve with baked potatoes and grilled asparagus or a green salad.

Community Theater at the Park

Submitted by Nancy Sager

When I was a child, back in the sixties, Parks and Recreation would perform skits at The Westgate Rec. Center. One year we did Froggy went a Courtin' and I played Miss Froggy. Family and friends all came to watch.

I also performed with the Hilltop Community Theater and have fond memories of those plays. I especially enjoyed when we performed at the Bean Dinners. I remember the first one was Music Man with the 1972 West High alumni. At the time, Blythe Ann Hitch was in charge of the production. Blythe Ann and her family were a big part of the formation of the Hilltop Community

Theater. They went on to perform many plays including *Lil Abner, King and I, Brigadoon, Oklahoma!, Fiddler on the Roof, Bye Bye Birdie* and many others. A personal note is I ended up playing a wall in one of the scenes of Brigadoon because of high winds.

I was honored to be a part of the Hilltop Community Theater board for a year. We actually had a yard sale in my yard to make money to put on these plays. By this time, the plays had moved to West High. The plays were expensive ventures but I believe everyone involved had a good time. They also put on children's plays for a period of time at Wedgewood School. They actually did one of those plays in the basement of Parkview United Methodist Church.

At Halloween we would spend hours decorating our jack-o-lanterns then we would dress up in costume and go over to Westgate Park and parade around the pond and through the woods with our lighted jack-o-lanterns.

Sledding to Westgate

As told to Sandy Whitehead by Linda Garvey

Linda now lives in Westgate but as a child in the late 1950s, she remembers winters when her Dad pulled her on a sled from across Sullivant to her aunt's home in Westgate. She remembers many hours spent flying kites in Westgate Park where the ball diamonds are now located.

Enjoying the Park

As told to Sandy Whitehead by Jim Iverson

Jim Iverson has lived in Westgate for eleven years. He likes to see activity in the park and enjoys the Westgate Neighbors Mugs & Muffins events.

He takes pride in the area and daily picks up trash in the park. He only wishes that others would feel the same way and pick up after themselves.

He loves the people of Westgate and especially enjoys the park. Jim says, "I would not live anywhere else!"

Above: *The ball fields in Westgate Park were the perfect spot for kite-flying in the summer. Photo by Beth Loughner.*
Top right: *Pat Buchner is all bundled up for some wintertime fun.* **Bottom right:** *Debbie Whitehead takes little brother Scott on a sled ride.*

Acrophobia!

As told to Debbie Maddox by Alexander Jones

Alex Jones has lived in the area for more than 15 years. One of his fondest memories is visiting Westgate Park's kiddie park back in the 1990s . Alex remembers the tall wooden playground equipment. The wooden structure had a center tower that connected to a slide and two swings that hung from a pole off the tower. Alex was very scared of the tower because he was afraid of heights but he really wanted to go down the slide. One day he got up the nerve to climb up the tower but once up there he was too scared to slide down. He finally got up the nerve and was surprised to learn how fast he slid down! Alex is disappointed that the wooden playground set has been replaced with a new, less scary model.

Future Lifeguard Takes His First Dip

As told to Betty Jaynes by Winnona W.

My memory of Westgate Park, on the surface, would seem to be an unpleasant one. In the mid-80's we attended a family reunion in the shelter house.

I had to run to the store for something, so I asked my Mom to watch my son Ray. At the time he was only 2 or 3 years old.

Imagine my horror when I returned to find the pond surrounded with emergency squads and fire trucks. As I rushed toward the scene I realized they were attending to Ray.

Ray had fallen into the pond and nearly drowned. I spent the next few weeks and months hugging him just a little tighter.

While his experience might have instilled a fear of water it actually had quite the opposite effect. Ray grew to love the water. So much so that he became a lifeguard at Glenwood Pool and a member of the swim team at Brookhaven.

I returned to the park in 2012 to watch my parents' band, Imani, perform at Westgate's Arts in the Park. As I looked towards the pond a flood of emotions came over me.

Ray is now 29 and in the Army. I have to wonder if he would have a love of water had he not nearly drowned that fateful day.

The Westgate Park water towers in 2012. Pilot Jerry Ziglar, photographer Bob Smith.

How Much For Your Hat, Mister?

As told to Sandy Whitehead by Pat Buchner

Pat grew up in house located on Parkside across from the park. During the 1950s Pat and her brother, along with friends, used Westgate Park as their playground.

She remembers well the Bean Dinners. Many hours were spent watching the men put together the rides and set up the booths for games. She loved the straw hats the men wore. One year she got the courage to ask a man for his hat. He told her if she brought him a cup of coffee, he would give her the hat. She brought him coffee in one of her mother's good china cups. Her mother was not happy but Pat got the hat. Christmas time was exciting when Santa came to the park.

Santa asks little Pat Buchner if she's been a good girl.

Pat and her brother work at snow removal.

My Wild Ride Down the Dirt Pile

As told to Sandy Whitehead by Charlotte & Stanton Prior

Stanton Prior remembers 1938 and the digging of two ponds in Westgate Park. The dirt was moved and piled into big mounds where the ball diamonds are now located. He and his friends loved riding their bikes down two of them. The third was very high and the boys felt it was too dangerous to ride down. One day Stanton built up his courage and climbed, with his bike, to the top of the hill. Halfway down, the bike went flying to the side and he tumbled the rest of the way down. He still sports the scar created by the wound he received on that wild ride!

Stanton also spoke about Ray Coffman who lived on Southampton, owned a Studebaker Company and had an optical business. Stanton got his glasses from Ray.

Carrot Lyonnaise

Submitted by Charlotte Prior

1 pound carrots
1 chicken bouillon cube
½ cup water
1 teaspoon salt
4 tablespoons butter
3 medium onions sliced
1 tablespoon flour
¾ cup water

This makes 6-8 servings and is Stanton's favorite!

1. Pare carrots and make 3 inch by ¼-inch strips.
2. Dissolve cube in ½ cup boiling water.
3. Add carrots and cook, covered, for 10 minutes.
4. Melt butter in skillet, add onions and cook 15 minutes stirring occasionally.
5. Add to onions the flour, salt, ¾-cup water and bring to a boil.
6. Add carrots and bouillon stock to onion mixture then simmer uncovered about 10 minutes or until carrots are tender.
7. Add a pinch of sugar before serving.

BUSINESSES

Haney's Economy Drug Store

Submitted by Judy (Rausch) Warner

Haney's Economy Drug Store was a neighborhood icon. Everyone knew about the drug store and came to meet, shop, eat or drink. I worked there for 6 years while I was in high school in the early 60s. My pay was 75 cents an hour when I started and got raises up to $1.35. Harry Haney Jr. was the store manager, pharmacist and a very good boss.

When I first started working at Haney's, I worked in the food/soda fountain area. It was fun visiting with all the people who came in. I learned how to make sodas, sundaes, flavored sodas, hamburgers, French fries and meals. My sodas were the best, and I can still make them! We had to wear white uniforms and aprons when we worked behind the fountain. When I worked the evening shift, I worked alone and was very busy at times. (I learned how to drink strong coffee when I worked at Haney's!) At night we only served drinks, sandwiches, fries and ice cream treats. Nighttime cleanup meant putting all the food items into the refrigerator, wiping everything down and cleaning the grill. What a horrible, messy job that was! You had to wipe and scrape it clean, then use a pumice stone to do the final cleaning. I also worked stock, inventory, and straightened things up. Working the register was another fun job.

I quit work after I got married and moved away. Some years later, there was a midnight fire and the store burned down and was never rebuilt.

Judy's Best Ice Cream Soda

Submitted by Judy Warner

Into a cold soda glass, place a dab of whipped cream. Pour seltzer water into the whipped cream and fill almost to the top. Then add two balls of ice cream; stir and enjoy.

Rausch Bros. Hardware

Submitted by Judy (Rausch) Warner

My dad, Lew Rausch, and his brother, Paul Rausch, went into the hardware business around 1929. The original hardware store, near the corner of W. Broad St. and Hague Ave., was called Broad Hague Hardware and was owned by two men named Burrier and Barrel. My dad was a senior at West High School when he began working there. Burrier asked my dad to quit school and work full time at the store but he decided to finish school and was in the first graduating class (1929) at the new West High School on Powell Ave. Dad then began his almost 40 year career in the hardware business. Uncle Paul quit his job at Packard Car Co. and began his partnership with dad and the store was renamed Rausch Bros. Hardware.

Murphy's Drug Store was next door to the hardware store, with a door between the two and a little hallway, which led to the shared stairway to the basement. My brother and I remember the stairway and basement as being dark and scary. In 1955, with business booming, Dad and Uncle Paul decided to enlarge the facility and constructed a new building a few doors down the street next to the Sohio Gas Station (where my uncle, Ivan Timmons, Sr., was station manager.) The new hardware store had a variety of departments: fish & tackle, hunting, paint, hardware, small appliances, bikes, Lionel trains, toys, farm and seed, and home repair, which included window glazing, glass cutting, screen repair, pipe threading, parts, tools, key making and locksmithing, and lots of "how to" information.

Geoff, my brother, who worked half days at the store while in high school, has favorite memories of the hardware store. He recalls having a frosty Coke on a Saturday morning from the old Coke machine, the neat Christmas train set-up in the front window of the store, and the night a phone call came to the house telling us that the huge fresh water aquarium located in one of the front windows had broken and the fish were flopping around on the floor. During Halloween, a window-painting contest was held for local businesses. Geoff and I painted the store windows every year. I think we were given ribbons as prizes. It was great fun.

Once Uncle Paul caught a thief — a lady wearing a huge coat. Uncle Paul was watching as she put a coffee pot inside her coat.

Rausch Brothers Hardware is two doors to the left of the restaurant. The building furthest on the left with the peaked roof is the Sohio Gas Station.

The police were called and she started crying but when they opened her coat they discovered that her coat was full of pockets with stuff she had taken.

Mr. Galbraith, from Galbraith's Farm in West Jefferson, was a customer of the store. Dad delivered something like 19,000 gallons of paint for the fences at Galbraith's. (Mr. Galbraith was an owner — along with Bing Crosby — of the Pittsburgh Pirates). Galbraith would hire the OSU football teams to paint the fences and rake the leaves. Galbraith built a large boat for the Pittsburgh Pirates football team to go on a boat outing — only to have it sink on the first venture!

Rausch Bros. Hardware did well until the discount stores came in and proceeded to undersell a lot of the hardware products. An auction was held in 1968 after almost 40 years of business.

Georgiton's Economy Drug Store

Submitted by Judy (Rausch) Warner

Georgiton's was located near the SW corner of Broad St. and Hague Ave., across from my dad's hardware store. My grandmother lived a few blocks south on Hague, and when I stayed overnight at her house, we would walk down to the store and buy one bottle of root beer and a pint of vanilla ice cream to make root beer floats when we got back home. We would sit on her front porch, drink our floats and watch the cars go by.

What could be better? When my neighborhood friends and I took Catechism Classes on Saturday mornings at St. John's Lutheran Church located on the other corner, we would always stop at Georgiton's afterward and buy two hot dog coneys and a coke for 25 cents. Georgiton's was a great gathering place.

The Hilltop Record
Of Interest to the People of the Hilltop and Vicinity

The Hilltop, Columbus, Ohio, Thursday, October 27, 1927.

Submitted by Johnny Steiner & Greg Harman

Favorite Recipe
BEER BREAD Easy as 1-2-3!

1 bottle of beer
2 tablespoons sugar
3 cups of self-rising flour

Combine ingredients.
Place in a prepared loaf pan.
Bake at 350 degrees for 25 minutes.
Remove.
Pour 2 TBSP melted margarine on top.
Return to oven for 25 more minutes.

YUM

** Try adding a bit of garlic or rosemary or cheese to the initial mixture

YUM-O!

Gearhart's Hardware – Where Service is Not Just Part of a Slogan

Submitted by Betty Jaynes

Special thanks to Dave Miller for his contribution to this story.

Mr. William Gearhart first opened his hardware store at the corner of Oakley and Sullivant in 1929. He later enlarged the store to allow for more merchandise.

When Mr. Gearhart died in 1946, his nephew, Jack Boyer, took over the store and installed the landmark sign – a gigantic hammer.

In 1989, Jack Boyer turned the store over to his nephew, Dave Miller – who began working in the store in 1966, when he was still in high school. As business continued to grow, Dave searched for a location that would offer a larger sales floor as well as better parking.

In 2003, Gearhart's moved to its current location at the corner of Roys and West Broad Street. Dave was hopeful that he could use the iconic sign, but was unable to secure the necessary permits.

He recently replaced a sign that was damaged in a storm. Going back to their roots, the new sign has a large hammer.

Dave shared that the recent downturn in the housing market has negatively affected sales, but he has started to see business slowly rebound.

He is encouraged by the many new young home buyers in the area. While the Westgate homes have charm, they also have unique fixtures and hardware. These new homeowners quickly find out that the big box stores do not offer the service, advice and experience found at Gearhart's.

Walk in with a plumbing part or a widget and Dave and his staff will know immediately the replacement part you need.

Good luck finding a single replacement screw at the big box store. At Gearhart's they can quickly identify the screw and tell you, "Oh, it's a cabinet hinge screw," and walk you to the back of the store and to the exact bin.

Need screens repaired or glass cut? If you head to the big box stores they will refer you right back to Gearhart's. In fact, Dave said that he gets calls every week from the big box stores asking if he carries a special product and they often ask him where they might find something in THEIR store.

While Dave does do a competitive store walk at Lowe's and Home Depot on a regular basis, it is his nearly half century of experience that has made him a Hardware Master.

So as Dave looks forward to retirement what are his plans for the store? His niece, Julie, who currently works in the store, has expressed interest in taking it over.

Dave said that while the business has remained in the extended family, none of its owners have ever had children. That explains why two nephews (and perhaps sometime in the future, a niece) have carried on the tradition of personal service and expert advice started by William Gearhart more than 80 years ago.

(Left): Photo of William Gearhart shortly after his original store opened on Sullivant Avenue in September 1929, just one month before the stock market crash. (Right): Newspaper clipping of the iconic sign at the Sullivant Avenue store coming down just after the W. Broad Street store opened in the Spring of 2003.

Advertising from Westgate area retail establishments. Various sources.

Girl Meets Storekeeper

Submitted by Steve Stone

It was in this store (see photo, opposite) that my mother and father met. My mother, Autumn Keefer, was a student at West High School. She and her girlfriends liked to roller-skate on newly paved streets in the Westgate neighborhood and would stop at the store for candy.

My dad ran the store and took a liking to the girl from West High. "I started to give her the candy for free so she would come back" he told me. They were married in 1936, raised a family on the Hilltop and remained together for well over 50 years. Mom and Dad often joked about what happened to her because she took candy from an "older" man.

Looking west, from the corner of West Broad Street and Hague Avenue in the 1950s.

This photograph of the grocery and gas station located at the corner of Sullivant and S. Huron Avenue was taken in 1931. The families of brothers Othmar and Carl Isselstein, who owned the business, changed their last name to "Stone" during World War II. Othmar's son and daughter-in-law, Steve and Jan Stone, live today on Crescent Drive. The store continued to operate under other owners until at least the 1970s. It was torn down in the early 2000s.

Haldeman Dry Cleaners – Keeping Westgate Clean For Over 75 Years

Submitted by Betty Jaynes

Special thanks to Mike Boehm for his contribution to this story.

Personal service – it is something in short supply at chains and big-box stores. Having been a customer of Haldeman Dry Cleaners for years, and after speaking with owner Mike Boehm, I can tell you "personal service and integrity" are not catch phrases – it is simply the way he runs his business.

Haldeman Dry Cleaners actually started in 1934 as Long and Haldeman Dry Cleaners at Eureka Avenue and West Broad Street. Owner Harley Haldeman, who lived in Westgate, relocated to 3115 West Broad Street sometime in the 1940s.

A fire caused major damage to the building and its contents in November, 1955. The fire burned for more than an hour. Three firemen suffered flash burns when a blast of smoke and fire shot at them from the inferno. They were knocked down by the force and suffered facial burns.

After the fire, Harley, and his brother Dick, moved the business to its current location – next door at 3117 West Broad Street.

Mike Boehm admits that even though he grew up in the dry cleaning business (his father was a tailor and later owned a store on the South End) that his life's dream after graduating from college was actually to become a pilot. He was in the Air Force Pilot training when he developed a

Customers would find advertising promos stuffed within the breast pocket of their suit jacket – complete with faux handkerchief.

heart condition and his dream was never fulfilled.

So, at 24, he came back to Columbus and what he knew – the dry cleaning business. When Mike bought the business in 1976 there were 13 Dry Cleaners on the West Side. He has outlasted all of them – including a Swan Cleaners location in Great Western.

He takes pride in his work and often washes or dry cleans garments multiple times to remove stains – at no extra cost to his customers. He and his staff empty pockets before cleaning garments. Items found are carefully put in an envelope to be returned to their owner. It costs him 3¢ for the envelope to return a penny, but he feels it is a matter of integrity and trust – and personal service.

"We found something in your pocket," he says as he shows a customer the envelope. "Were you missing a $1,000 bill? If you were, you still are," he often quips.

After 36 years he can honestly say that he still enjoys coming to work. Sure, the business has been challenging, but he cherishes the many, lasting relationships he has built with the people of Westgate. He has no plans to retire soon – in fact he recently installed a new sign for the front of his business.

Oh, and the strangest thing left in a pocket…. a dead mouse!!! Not sure if that was returned to its rightful owner.

The Leaman Building

Submitted by Jackie Litteral

Dr. Leaman and his wife built the multi-purpose building at 3181 West Broad.

Mrs. Leaman loved to dance and she held dances in the hallways. There are several apartments in the building and at one time businesses were located in the basement.

Jackie Litteral's first beauty shop was in one of the business areas and an alterations business in another.

Mrs. Leaman had hoped one day to convert the entire building into an apartment complex for senior citizens. Those plans never materialized but it remains a rental apartment building.

Schoedinger Hilltop Chapel

Submitted by Betty Jaynes

Special thanks to Andrea Stockel, manager of the Hilltop Chapel, for her contribution to this story.

In 1855 the Schoedinger family opened a single downtown funeral chapel in Columbus. Since then, this historic local business has been handed down through six generations to become Schoedinger Funeral and Cremation Service with fourteen chapels throughout Central Ohio.

Encouraged by growth on the Hilltop, they purchased the Floyd-Born Funeral Home and opened their first branch at the corner of Richardson Avenue and West Broad Street in 1950.

In 1955 they began working with local real estate developer Cliff Rice, to build at their current location. In 1997 they updated their façade by adding a pitched roof.

Beyond supporting the Westgate community as a funeral home, Schoedinger has many important outreach programs. In 1996 they created their Annual Candlelight Memorial Service. Recognizing that the holidays can be an extremely difficult time for families that have experienced a loss in the past year, the Schoedinger Family and Associates invite these families to a candlelight memorial service. It is a time of healing, and a time to honor and remember lost loved ones. They also sponsor Senior Health Fairs and grief programs at local churches.

As a pillar of the Hilltop for nearly six decades, Schoedinger Funeral and Cremation Service is a long standing member of the Hilltop Business Association, supports the annual Hilltop Bean Dinner, Friends of the Hilltop Beautification Awards, and our very own Westgate Home and Garden Tour.

We thank them for their continued support of Westgate.

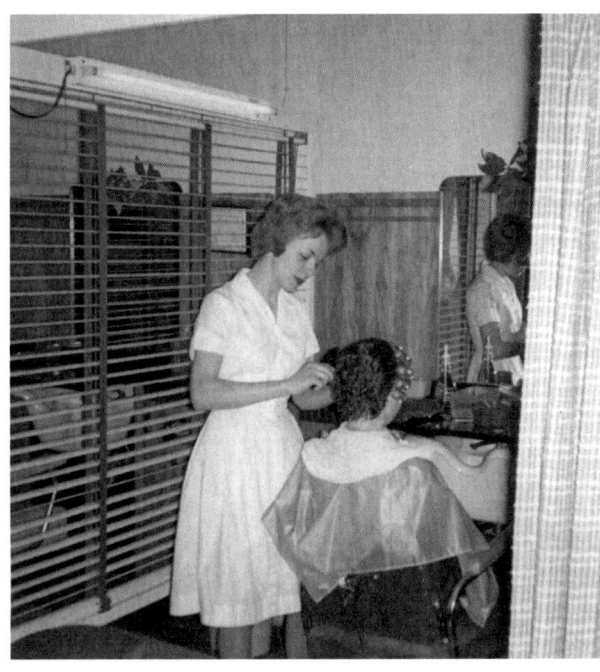

Getting a wash and set at the "beauty parlor" was a weekly routine for many housewives during the 1950s and 60s.

Westmoor Beauty Salon – Where Beauty is Ageless

Submitted by Betty Jaynes

Special thanks to Connie Kaufman for her contribution to this story.

Perhaps you've wondered why the salon at the corner of South Westgate Avenue and West Broad Street was named Westmoor Beauty Salon. Mr. Mohler, who originally owned the salon, lived on Westmoor. When he retired, he sold the business to Leora Betsch. Connie Kaufman went to work for Leora when she graduated from beauty school in 1961.

When Connie bought the business from Leora in 1965, she shortened the name from Mohler's Westmoor Beauty Salon to just Westmoor Beauty Salon.

At one time there were seven hairdressers working at the salon. Even as hairstyles changed, Connie and Millie Gentile-Reed had a very loyal clientele.

Connie was known for her elaborate seasonal window displays.

In the 1990's she won the Best Business Holiday Display sponsored by the Hilltop Business Association (HBA).

Speaking of the HBA, Connie was active in the Association and was the first elected woman president.

Connie and Millie continued to serve their clients to the very end. And by that I mean they would pack up their rollers, combs and hairspray, and travel to Jerry Spears and Schoedinger Funeral Homes to do one final wash and set. I asked Connie how she was able to do it and she said, "At first, it was a bit unsettling, but after a few times Millie and I realized it was one final thing we could do for our clients. These women wanted the same hair style every week – we didn't need a picture – we knew exactly what they would want."

Westmoor Beauty Salon was one of the last shops that still did roller sets and most clients had a standing weekly appointment. I know how much my mother looked forward to "hair day."

Sadly, many of the original clients have passed away or moved into assisted living facilities. Millie retired in 2008 and Connie closed the shop in 2009. Connie wanted to continue serving the women she had seen weekly for decades. She now works a few days a week at "The Aristocrat" at the corner of Wayne and W. Mound.

Holiday window display at Westmoor Beauty Salon.

Formation Studio

Submitted by Mari Ann Binder Futty

Alan Jazak left his position at Chute Gerdeman to begin his own graphic design business on July 4, 2001. Since his personal independence day coincided with the U.S. holiday, Alan did the only logical thing and took the day off.

Since that day – well, since the day after that day – Alan has been turning vision into reality through the use of design. "When my clients see a finished product and I can see the pride in their eyes, that's what matters most to me." When he worked in the larger corporate world, he sat on project committees, never seeing the company owners. Now he works directly with small companies and entrepreneurs. "I know I'm changing their business, their life."

Alan is quick to point out that he is not just a business owner – he is the artistic director for his company. That artistic, creative edge comes across in the Formation Studio name and logo. Alan said that when designing a logo, web page, advertisement, program or brochure layout, he is forming – or transforming information into – a product. "Also, if you think about things being in a formation, as in, ducks in a row, things are in their place for a purpose, a reason – by design!" As for the logo, even "out of the box" isn't adequate in describing Alan and his work. His logo is an open box on fire.

For someone with so much creativity, it's not surprising that his favorite projects are related to the arts. "I have a big place in my heart for those projects." In addition to paying clients such as the Columbus Arts Festival, Alan has done pro bono work for many arts groups including the Columbus Film Council and the Columbus Gay Men's Chorus. "I like event promotions because they change so often … show to show, season to season, year to year. I never get bored."

Formation Studio has always been located in Alan's house in Westgate. After working out of one of the bedrooms for three years, he put in a bid on a downtown condominium. When he lost the bid, he saw that as a sign. "I decided that whatever I was going to put into the move to the condo, I would put into the house," he said. He built an addition on his second floor, and created a covered patio in the backyard space beneath the new office.

His home now has just one bedroom, but boasts two office spaces – the one he built onto the house being large enough for himself, his office manager and a conference area/work table.

Adding more workspace allowed Alan to increase his vision for his company and staff. "Putting on the addition changed my perspective of what the business could become," he said. He added a website programmer, allowing him to add website creation and design to his menu of services. At its busiest, Formation Studio generated more than enough work to keep Alan, three full-time employees and an intern busy.

Even with all of that, he couldn't resist helping out the neighborhood. "The first thing that made me feel connected to Westgate was when I got a letter asking me to donate to the fountain (building project) for the pond in Westgate Park." He added, "That's when I knew I was in a neighborhood. I remember going to see the fountain, thinking that I helped make that." When the Westgate Neighbors Association formed, he jumped right on the bandwagon, and since then has been doing everything from sitting on planning committees to putting his house on two home tours to donating mountains of design work. From the home and garden tour logo, program books and promotional materials, Arts in the Park flyers and banners, to the website and promotional video, to the design and layout of this book, Alan's professional touch is on nearly everything produced by the WNA. He's never said no to a project, never lost his patience with over zealous committee chairmen and board members, and never ever lost his creativity, passion and enthusiasm for Westgate. "It reminds me of the neighborhood I grew up in, in Cleveland. It feels like home."

Beck and Orr

Submitted by Betty Jaynes

Special thanks to Ron Bowman for his contribution to this story.

Don't ask Ron Bowman, owner of Beck and Orr, if he owns a Kindle or Nook. His life is books, real books – I guess you could call him "The Book Doctor."

On work tables dating back to the 1800s, Ron and his son Skip respectfully restore family Bibles, baptismal journals, genealogies and old much-loved children's books.

Hand case book binding books is very labor intensive. While they have century-old machinery, much of the work is done by hand. Hot foil stamping is done with type templates over 80 years old.

Beck and Orr is the only company in central Ohio that specializes in bookbinding services for volumes old and new. In addition to restoration work, a large portion of their work is thesis binding for OSU and the College of Art and Design.

"We've done books that have gone to the White House and projects that have gone to the Vatican," said Ron. "The oldest book I ever worked on was a Bible from 1437."

Beck and Orr started as a family business in 1888 in downtown Columbus. They moved several times, twice as a result of devastating fires. Ron and his wife Loretta bought out the last remaining family member in the early 1980s. It was Loretta who encouraged Ron to rebuild after a fire gutted the business in 1990. That move brought the business to Westgate. Ron, a graduate of West High School and a resident of Westgate, moved to his current location on West Broad Street just blocks from his home.

The hand-cranked presses, an enormous cutter and a sewer – all in use for over a century – are the core of Beck and Orr. But it is Ron who is the heart of the business. He is a true master craftsman.

Pictured above is Ron Bowman with his cutting machine that dates back to 1930. The special edition hard-bound copies of this publication are an example of the work done by Beck and Orr.

NOTABLE PEOPLE

Westgate Politicians and Public Servants

Submitted by Betty Jaynes

Several neighborhood residents have served in public office and as judges — three mayors alone have come from Westgate!

Many more residents have run for elected office, desiring to serve on the School Board, on City Council, and even at the State House.

Each Halloween, our current Mayor, Mike Coleman, visits Westgate on Trick or Treat night. His first stop is Lori Bowman-Garrard's home on Westmoor. He has a couple bowls of her famous chili and visits around the bonfire before heading out to see the many homes decorated for Halloween. He says he loves the area and enjoys passing out candy to the children.

Mayor Michael B. Coleman begins Halloween at the home of Lori Bowman-Garrard.

Mayor Floyd F. Green

Submitted by Betty Jaynes and John Futty

Sources: The Columbus Dispatch, the Columbus Citizen-Journal and Franklin County auditor

Floyd F. Green lived at 3046 Crescent Dr. during his one term in the mayor's office, 1940–1943. Franklin County auditor's records show that he and his wife, Esther, were the original occupants of the Westgate home, purchasing it in December 1926. They were still living there when the former mayor died in January 1952 at the age of 52.

Green also served on Columbus City Council from 1927 to 1931. He won the 1939 mayoral election with the slogan, "Get out of the red with Green."

As mayor, he accompanied President Franklin D. Roosevelt when he visited Columbus to dedicate Poindexter Village in October 1940 and inspected the city's first air-raid sirens in the days after the attack on Pearl Harbor in December 1941.

But his term was marred by controversy, beginning with questions about "the speedy repayment of a mortgage against his Crescent Dr. home, which he negotiated Oct. 6, 1939, ostensibly to

finance his successful campaign," according to a *Columbus Dispatch* story. "The mortgage was for $2,750, to be paid over a 10-year period. His campaign expenses were formally reported at $8,820. He took office on Jan. 1, 1940. The mortgage was cancelled as paid on Oct. 6 that year."

He also was dogged by claims that he used city employees to plant trees and do other chores at the Madison County farm he purchased in 1942.

But the biggest stain on his term was a gambling scandal in the city that led to a scathing grand-jury report criticizing the leadership of the police department for looking the other way.

Repudiated by his own party in his bid for re-election, he was defeated in the 1943 Republican primary by a rising star, future governor James A. Rhodes.

Green was one of the most persistent mayoral candidates the city has ever known. He ran for the office in 1931 and 1935 before his only victory in 1939. He also made unsuccessful bids for mayor in 1947 and 1951—all while a resident of Westgate.

Mayor Maynard Edward "Jack" Sensenbrenner

Submitted by Betty Jaynes

Thanks to Dick Sensenbrenner, the Mayor's son, for his contribution to this story.

No book about Westgate would be complete without a story about one of its most famous residents, Mayor Sensenbrenner

Jack was born in Circleville, Ohio in 1902, and after living in California for a few years he returned to Ohio and settled first on Ogden Avenue. He and his wife, Mildred, moved to Westgate to raise their family, living at 335 Guernsey Avenue from the mid 1940s until 1967.

Jack was very active in his church, Hoge Memorial Presbyterian – serving as deacon and elder and teaching the largest adult Sunday school class in Ohio. He was President of the Hilltop Kiwanis and a lifelong member of the Hilltop Business Association. He was very active in Big Brothers, Boy Scouts, YMCA, and West High Boosters as well as several other civic organizations.

In 1953 members of the Council of Churches and Hilltop business leaders encouraged Jack to run for Mayor. Columbus had not had a Democratic mayor since 1935, so his upset win – by less than 400 votes – made national news.

Jack was the first candidate to use television to reach out to voters. Jack credited his win to the hard work and support of the residents of the Westside and the members of Hoge Memorial Church.

Jack was a tireless champion of the City of Columbus and his country. He was known to always have a pocket full of USA Flag lapel pins – with Columbus, Ohio across the bottom. His other pocket would be full of USA Flag rings for the ladies and candy bars for the kids. Jack never met a stranger and was an outstanding ambassador for our "All American City" wherever he traveled.

Jack laid the groundwork for the massive growth of Columbus in the late 20th century by requiring that all neighborhoods accepting city water service first be annexed into the city. Under his leadership the city grew from 40 square miles in 1950 to 142 square miles in 1970. Today, thanks to Mayor Sensenbrenner's vision, the city encompasses more than 200 square miles.

In his first term, Jack and his cabinet put together "Metropolitan Housing" for low-income people and senior citizens, developed the Columbus recreation and parks system, and put the Columbus Zoo on the path to becoming a national attraction.

His Circleville High School Football Coach Ivan Davis (Jack earned a letter as the water boy) would yell coming into the locker room, "what you guys need is a good shot of some spizzerinctum"— a quality that was 1000 times greater than enthusiasm. Jack adopted the term, and by all accounts, the attitude.

Jack was a very popular visionary Democratic Mayor of Columbus from 1954–1960 and 1964–1972, and a proud resident of Westgate from the mid 1940s until 1967 when he and Mildred moved into a one-story home in North Columbus.

In 1992 a memorial to Mayor Sensenbrenner was erected at "the top of the hill" in Glenwood Park on West Broad Street. It honors a man whose creed of "God, Love and Country" helped to win Columbus the coveted "All American Award" from the National Civic League in 1958.

Mayor W. Ralston Westlake

Submitted by Betty Jaynes

W. Ralston Westlake (1907–1978) served as the 47th Mayor of Columbus, Ohio from 1960–1963.

He was born on South Highland Avenue, graduated from West High School in 1925, and continued living on the Hilltop throughout his life.

As an adult, he lived in a two story home located at 3294 West Broad Street where he also owned a small motel and the Westlake Ruby Glass Studio.

The property was later sold and the vacant land behind it was converted to self storage units and the motel units were converted to small offices.

Bea Murphy, Westgate Treasure

Submitted by Kathy Seibert and Beth Chamberlin

We love living in Westgate, but what makes Westgate special is less about the place than it is about the people who live within this rich and diverse community.

Beth and I have lived on the northwest corner of Binns and Fremont for almost 15 years. We love the park, the library, our friends at Westgate United Methodist Church, the Rec center, the WNA and our police and fire departments. We love our neighbors, our block watches, our walks through the neighborhood in every kind of weather with our two dogs; taking in a show by "Bread and Circus Theatre," and getting together with friends and neighbors once a month to play euchre. We love Halloween in Westgate, where — judging by the great number of ghosts, goblins, superheroes, villains, princesses and fairies and every other costume-wearing child within the 270 outerbelt — others do as well!

One of the most special and amazing things to us about Westgate, however, is the person we are blessed to live right beside and call our friend and neighbor – Bea Murphy. Bea was born in Huntington, Alabama in 1939 and spent time picking cotton in the cotton fields ... but that's another story. Bea has lived in Westgate since 1985 and has made a significant imprint not only in Westgate, but in the surrounding communities as well.

Bea is a living historian with a wealth of knowledge she freely shares in her desire to educate and promote the neighborhood of Westgate in which she lives and loves. She has served on the boards of several organizations such as the Franklinton and Hilltop Historical Societies and our own Camp Chase just to name a few. Bea can be found at the Hilltop Bean Dinner every year sharing her stories with all who will listen on a variety of historical topics. Bea has been involved with the Westland Flea Market (and others) for 20 years and is currently the market's entertainment co-coordinator.

In 1995, Bea and her family were seriously impacted when an object was thrown from an overpass. She worked tirelessly and was instrumental in the passage of House Bill 179, which made the act illegal.

In 1997, Bea conducted research for the Franklinton Bicentennial Celebration, which led to the discovery of Arthur Boke, Jr., who is believed to be the first African American who lived in Franklinton — possibly in the city of Columbus. Bea went on to raise funds to have Bokes' gravesite, located in Greenlawn Cemetery, repaired. She also met Alfred Tibor, a world-renowned sculptor, and from that meeting came the "Celebration of Life" statue, which is a tribute to Boke. The statue is located near the West Broad Street Bridge. Bea petitioned and received over $35,000 in donations to build the statue from local businesses, and the remaining $10,000 was donated by people right here in Westgate and surrounding communities. What stuck out in my mind was when Bea told me about the homeless man in Westgate Park who gave her a quarter toward the building of the statue. Here was a person obviously of little means who believed enough in what she was doing to offer her what little he had, and Bea in turn dignified the man by accepting his gift. There is a red oak tree in front of the Westgate Recreation Center that Bea planted 12 years ago in honor of Boke. Look for it and read the plaque at the base of the tree the next time you're out for a walk.

Bea regularly cleans and tends to the statue honoring Arthur Boke, Jr.

In 2005, Bea held a poetry reading in her garden. The sculptor she worked with on the Boke statue attended, along with his wife and several other Westgate poets and artists.

Bea was a 1995 "Women of Character" nominee; she is an award-winning poet and songwriter, an author and singer. She wrote and recorded "Ode to the Harley": She was inspired on one of her walks through Westgate Park by a man riding a Harley Davidson motorcycle with a big flag blowing in the wind as he was riding west into the setting sun. Beth and I still expect to see Bea pull up in front of her house someday wearing leather and climbing off her "hog"!

She is presently working on a biography of Arthur Boke, Jr., and the Ohio State University interviews her periodically regarding her historical research on Boke.

Bea can be found on any given day walking around Westgate as she logs four plus miles a day. At 73 years young, these two friends and neighbors can tell you she's an inspiration and role model for any neighborhood.

When asked to sum up her impression of Westgate and this community she lives in, she responded: "Love people – I meet no strangers." Well said, Bea. Well said!

The Westgate Neighbors Association (WNA) hosted a dedication ceremony on March 19, 2011 to unveil the monument signs placed on the neighborhood's perimeter to identify Westgate and to welcome visitors. The sign on West Broad Street is located at South Roys Avenue, and the two signs on Sullivant Avenue are at South Powell Avenue and Demorest Road.

Above: Mayor Michael Coleman (left) attended the ceremony. He is pictured along with Mari Ann Binder Futty, WNA president (center) and Adero Robinson, senior impact director for the United Way of Central Ohio (right).

Below: Residents braved the chilly March weather for the unveiling. The United Way awarded two Neighborhood Partnership Grants to the WNA to build and place the signs.

Senator Kerry's Front Porch Summit

Submitted by Betty Jaynes

The 2004 Presidential election put the national spotlight on Westgate when Senator John Kerry ran for president against incumbent George W. Bush. Senator Kerry's motorcade drove south on Demorest, headed toward a campaign rally at Westgate Park.

Before the rally, Senator Kerry held a "Front Porch Summit" at the home of Lynette Farmer on Wicklow. Lynette and her sister, Lori Bowman-Garrard – both single mothers – were selected for an informal discussion with Senator Kerry.

According to Lori, the entire family had to go through a background check and Lynette's home got the once-over by specially trained dogs. The Secret Service swept the home and surrounding area one final time an hour before the Senator arrived.

While the visit lasted only a half hour, Lori said that Senator Kerry showed genuine concern about the challenges facing single mothers. He tossed a football with the kids before walking with the family to the park for the rally.

Left, Lynette Farmer; Center, Senator John Kerry; Right, Lori Bowman-Garrard.

After the rally the motorcade left the park and drove north on Westgate to the cheers of – based on the outcome of the election – nearly half the residents of Westgate.

Lori, of course, wishes the outcome of the election had been different, as they would have been invited to attend one of the Inaugural Balls.

Lynette, who passed away in 2008, felt honored to have been selected to speak live from Tommy's Diner via satellite to the 2004 National Democratic Convention.

Cheese, Squash And Onion Galette

Submitted by Patti Von Niessen

Dough:
- 1 cup flour
- 1/8 tsp. salt
- 1/8 tsp. sugar
- 6 T (3/4 stick) unsalted butter, very cold, cut into small slices
- 1/4 cup ice water

Filling:
- 1 tbsp olive oil
- 1/2 onion, thinly sliced
- 2 yellow squash, sliced into 1/4-inch rounds
- 1 tbsp fresh thyme, or 1-1/2 teaspoons dried thyme
- salt and pepper to taste
- ½ cup Asiago cheese (grated)
- 1 tbsp milk or cream

To make the Dough:

In a large bowl, mix the flour, salt, and sugar. Using a pastry blender, cut the chilled butter into the flour mixture just until the butter is the size of crumbs.

Make a well in the middle of the dough. Pour a small amount of ice water into the center, and using a fork, bring some of the flour-butter mixture into the water. Continue until all of the water has been well incorporated. The mixture will be slightly crumbly, but it should hold together. If it does not, add more cold water, 1 tablespoon at a time. Press the dough into a ball and then flatten it into a disk about 5 inches in diameter. Wrap in plastic wrap and refrigerate for 2 to 24 hours. The dough can be frozen.

To make the Filling:

Preheat the oven to 400°F. In a medium skillet, heat the olive oil over medium-high heat; add the onions, squash, and sauté for about 2 minutes, stirring constantly. Add thyme, salt, and pepper, continue to cook until the onions and squash are translucent, but not brown, about 5 minutes. They should be slightly underdone. Remove from the heat and set aside.

To assemble

Remove the dough from the refrigerator, and on a well-floured surface or floured piece of parchment, roll into a circle 9 inches in diameter. Place the dough in a shallow baking or pizza pan.

Spoon the onion-squash mixture onto the center of the dough, leaving a 1-1/2-inch border. Top with the cheese. Next, fold the 1-1/2 inch border of the galette toward the center to encase part of the filling, crimping the edges a little, as you go. You should end up with a "window" of filling about 5 inches in diameter, with the crust overlapping the edges of the filling. Brush the folded-over edges with the milk or cream.

Bake until the crust is golden brown and the cheese is bubbly, 25 to 30 minutes. Serve immediately.

THE CLASSIC SALAD NIÇOISE

RECIPE FROM KEN WRIGHT

This recipe appeared in the Westgate Home and Garden Tour Program Book in 2012.

For the Vinaigrette

2 tsp white wine vinegar

3/4 cup extra-virgin olive oil

1 teaspoon honey

1 medium shallot, minced

1 Tbsp minced fresh thyme leaves

2 Tbsp minced fresh basil leaves

2 teaspoons minced fresh oregano leaves

1 teaspoon Dijon mustard

Salt and freshly ground black pepper

For the Salad

2 grilled or otherwise cooked tuna steaks (8 oz each)

6 hard-boiled eggs, peeled and either halved or quartered

10 small new red potatoes (each about 2 inches in diameter, about 1 1/4 pounds total), each potato scrubbed and quartered

Salt and freshly ground black pepper

2 medium heads Boston lettuce or butter lettuce, leaves washed, dried, and torn into bite-sized pieces

3 small ripe tomatoes, cored and cut into eighths

1 small red onion, sliced very thin

8 ounces green beans, stem ends trimmed and each bean halved crosswise

1/4 cup niçoise olives

2 Tbsp capers, rinsed or several anchovies (optional)

1) Marinate tuna steaks in a little olive oil for an hour. Heat a large skillet on medium high heat, or place on a hot grill. Cook the steaks 2 to 3 minutes on each side until cooked through.

2) Whisk vinegar, oil, shallot, thyme, basil, oregano, and mustard in medium bowl; season to taste with salt and pepper and set aside.

3) Bring potatoes and 4 quarts cold water to boil in a large pot. Add 1 tablespoon salt and cook until potatoes are tender, 5 to 8 minutes. Transfer potatoes to a medium bowl with a slotted spoon (do not discard boiling water). Toss warm potatoes with 1/4 cup vinaigrette; set aside.

4) While potatoes are cooking, toss lettuce with 1/4 cup vinaigrette in large bowl until coated. Arrange lettuce on a serving platter. Cut tuna into 1/2-inch thick slices, coat with vinaigrette. Mound tuna in center of lettuce. Toss tomatoes, red onion, 3 tablespoons vinaigrette, and salt and pepper to taste in bowl; arrange tomato-onion mixture on the lettuce bed. Arrange reserved potatoes in a mound at edge of lettuce bed.

5) Return water to boil; add 1 tablespoon salt and green beans. Cook until tender-crisp, 3 to 5 minutes. Drain beans, transfer to ice water, and let stand until just cool, about 30 seconds; dry beans well. Toss beans, 3 tablespoons vinaigrette, and salt and pepper to taste; arrange in a mound at edge of lettuce bed.

6) Arrange hard-boiled eggs, olives, and anchovies in mounds on the lettuce bed. Drizzle eggs with remaining 2 tablespoons dressing, sprinkle entire salad with capers and serve immediately.

GARDENS & PETS

Mary's Garden of Memories

Submitted by Mary Walsh

My maternal grandfather loved flowers and was an avid gardener of all growing things. My mother took after Pa's love of gardening and kept his memories alive with hollyhocks by the old privy. Back years ago people would plant hollyhocks, sweet peas, and blue morning glories around their privies. Whenever I see any of those plants, I remember the outhouses across the lands.

One thing I remember about my dad, he planted a garden each year. During the depression he planted more than usual, sold what he could and gave away to those who were broke. He was a good-hearted man.

I was always awaiting spring; it was so much fun going mushroom hunting with my father and mother. Sometimes I would dig up a wildflower or two. I have wildflowers in my little north side flowerbed: violets, sweet William, Jack in the pulpit, Virginia blue bells, Jacobs ladder, hellebore, bleeding heart, hardy geranium, forget-me-nots, and ferns. It is a joy to glance out my window to spot the first flower of the spring.

The flowers that really make the yard sing are my antique poppies and the faithful larkspurs. Those seeds are from Pa's farm and our home when I was a little girl. I gather seeds each year, just in case someone would like some.

The raised garden bed allows Mary to tend to her flowers from her wheelchair.

One of my dearest friends gave me starts of her mini purple iris, a small pink rose, and best of all, seeds from her antique petunias. Anne is no longer on this earth but I am sure that she watches over her flowers and me. Anne gave me lily of the valley starts for all seven places I have lived since the early 1970's.

As sure as I am writing this, I am sure that gardening is what has kept me sane. It was hard for me to accept my paralysis because I figured I would never be the same without my "digging legs." I have more weeds than before but I do try to do what I can. One of the ironic things, I became paralyzed on the first day of summer 1996!

Jack & Katie, Neighborhood Socialites

Submitted by Kerry and Susan Reeds

Our dogs, Katie a Yellow Lab, and Jack an Australian Blue Healer, love Westgate almost as much as we do.

During their many walks, they enjoy meeting the other canine residents. We have met many of our neighbors through their dogs – in fact Kerry is known as "Katie's dad."

Jack, the more vocal of the two, likes to make his presence known and warns visitors when they get too close to his territory. We didn't realize how often we yell at him to stop barking until an "alley picker" …or should I say….."recycler"….was heard to say "Shut up Jack !!"

Customers of Whole Goodness Bread look forward to Tuesdays when Patti Von Niessen delivers orders of fresh baked goods on her candy apple red bicycle, "The Madonna."

Here Kitty, Kitty, Kitty!

Submitted by Bob Waddell and Patti Von Niessen

While packing the car for a weekend away, our cat "Tea" snuck out. When we came back and realized she wasn't around, we tore apart the attic walls and opened the furnace vents to make certain she hadn't gone in, looking for a warm spot to curl up. After satisfying ourselves that she was nowhere in the house, we put up "Missing Kitty" signs around the neighborhood and walked the streets calling her name. After three days of fretting, it was time to think like a cat. We put her litter box, climbing tower, the blankets she frequently laid on, and some of our favorite sweaters outside. We then lit a fire in the fireplace to complete our creation of a Tea-full "sniff zone', and it worked! She came running home in about 15 minutes … probably thinking we were either trying to help her find her way, or were tossing her out for good!

Good Boy! Biscuits

Submitted by Rex Barker

2 cups unbleached white flour

½ cup wheat germ

½ cup nutritional yeast
(better for me than brewer's yeast)

2 teaspoons garlic powder
(better for me than fresh garlic)

3 tablespoons vegetable oil

1 cup chicken or beef stock.
(Or squirrel. Or rabbit. Retrievers may want to go with duck or pheasant stock.)

{ Yes, this is a real recipe for dog treats that repel fleas.
(That's what the yeast and garlic is all about.) }

Wash your paws. Have your human preheat the big hot box in the food room to 400 degrees and grease a cookie sheet or two.

Combine flour, wheat germ and yeast in a bowl; in a separate bowl mix the oil and garlic powder. Alternately add oil mixture and the stock to the flour mixture until all the ingredients are mixed together into a smooth dough. Warning: If you slobber too much into the bowl, you have to reduce the amount of stock you put in, so try to control yourself.

Roll over the dough – oh wait – that's wrong. Roll out the dough on a floured surface to ¼ inch thickness, cut into shapes (kitty-cat shapes taste the best), put on the cookie sheet and put the cookie sheet into the hot box.

Take yourself for a 20-25 minute walk. When you get back, have your human turn off the hot box, but leave the biscuits inside for a few hours to cool and dry out.

Favorite Recipe from Jerry Johnson:

Garden Whipps

1 part Pinnacle Whipped (flavored vodka)
3 parts sweetened lemonade or orange soda
– Ice –
Goes down smooth and 2 or 3 will make any garden look like paradise!

Originally printed in the 2011 Westgate Home & Garden Tour booklet.

It's a family affair for Buckley (right) and his sister Lilly (left). Buckley lives with Sandy and Lou Whitehead, while Lilly lives with Sandy and Lou's daughter and son-in-law, Debbie and Shawn Maddox.

Dandelion Salad

Submitted by Tony and Roma Painter

4 cups fresh dandelion greens
¾ cup shredded mozzarella cheese
2 large Portabella mushrooms (sliced)
4 Tbsp olive oil
½ cup thinly sliced red onion
2 Tbsp wine vinegar
1 cup cherry tomatoes

Toss all ingredients together and season to taste with fresh basil, salt and pepper.

Be Careful What You Plant

Submitted by Jerry & Betty Jaynes

Our neighbor, who was raised in the home across the street from us and later moved back when his mother passed away, shared this picture. He believes it dates back to the 1940s. The photo was taken shortly after the previous owners of our house had planted what they had to believe was a magnolia bush.

Years later our magnolia TREE still graces our front yard. While it is indeed beautiful – for about 2 ½ days during the spring – it is not a tree we would have chosen for our front yard.

The blossoms are quite slippery when wet and tend to stain the driveway. If we have an early frost the buds litter our driveway. Fall of course brings the leaves. It seems as if we are forever cleaning up after it.

However, it does provide wonderful shade and about once every five years, when the weather is just perfect, we enjoy the fragrant blossoms of a tree in full bloom.

Drive around Westgate in the spring and you will see several Magnolia trees. They must have been very popular in the 1940s.

The Blizzard of '78

Submitted by Carl and Marie Gillogly

I grew up on the Westside and spent a lot of time at Westgate Park. I especially enjoyed ice skating in the winter and the Bean Dinner. After Marie and I were married and ready to buy our first home we were drawn to Westgate.

We moved into our home in the spring of 1977. Fortunately we had the forethought to buy a snow shovel as our first winter would bring the worst winter storm in Ohio history.

Shortly before dawn on Thursday, January 26, 1978 the "Great Blizzard" hit. It continued through Thursday and into Friday. In addition to the bitter cold we had winds of 50 to 70 mph causing lots of drifting snow.

Around 10:30 Thursday night we heard a loud cracking sound and then an enormous crash. When we looked out our window we saw our neighbor's 40' pine tree had been uprooted by the wind and had fallen across Westgate Ave. into the neighbor's yard across the street. Around midnight we heard chain saws and saw a city crew cutting the center out of the tree, throwing the cut pieces into the yards. This opened up Westgate Ave. to traffic. Westgate Ave needed to be open because Westgate Rec. Center was being used as a relief center for anyone needing shelter.

We woke up in the morning to a loud noise and looked out to see an articulating farm tractor with a blade on the front clearing Westgate Ave. It was several days after the storm before all of the side streets in the Westgate neighborhood were cleared of the snow.

Fortunately, we didn't lose power during the storm. Over the next few days – with school out and many businesses closed – the younger neighbors spent hours digging out their elderly neighbors. We also enjoyed the shopping trip to Big Bear on Broad St. using the sled to bring our groceries home.

It was a very memorable first winter in our new home.

Dottie The Dalmatian Speaks Out

As told to Betty Jaynes by Dottie the dog

(With my humans, Paul and Jennifer Adams)

I moved to Westgate in 2005. I didn't have much say in the decision, but I can tell you I sure do like the place. We, and by we I mean Paul, wanted a home that he could work on and didn't want a cookie cutter neighborhood.

I do like the neighborhood, but the park is my favorite – I spend lots of time there with Paul. I don't have to bother with a leash as I understand and obey voice commands. Some say that I am the most obedient dog they know. What they don't know is that I have my owners well trained.

Many people know Paul as "Dottie's Dad" – as it should be. I mean, as any pet parent knows, you exist to pamper and protect us.

My Mom (Jennifer) makes very warm coats for me to wear. We moved from Georgia, so I am still not keen on these Ohio winters.

Some might know me from Facebook. I have been featured on the pages of Friends of Westgate Park and Westgate Arts in the Park.

Of course, being part Dalmatian, I am often mistaken as a movie star. In fact one day, shortly after the movie 101 Dalmatians came out, a group of kids asked my Mom if I was one of them. Not wanting to burst their bubble she told them I was number 98. They squealed with delight as they ran to tell their mother that they had just met #98.

So, if you see me out walking stop and say "Hi." If you happen to have a Milkbone in your pocket, you would make my day.

The Blizzard Killed My Old Friend

By Sally Yocom

We LOST AN old friend in the Blizzard of '78. It happened in the middle of the night, while the wind whirled and roared with the fury of a river crashing through a broken dam.

As I lay trembling, I grew aware of another sound, an eerie sound, which increased in intensity even over the savage howling of the blizzard, the creaking walls and the rattling windows. It seemed to be the groaning of a living thing in agony; it was a heart-wrenchingly mournful moaning, and it came from our front yard.

I slipped out of bed, shivering, and peered through the window. Great clouds of snow were being tossed about like clothes in a dryer, but there was no sign of human or animal. I climbed back into bed.

The terrible groaning continued. Were the eaves complaining about their heavy load of snow? Another groan, a longer one, filled the room with trembling waves of anguish, followed by a soft, rustling sound. Silence. The snow must have fallen from the eaves.

I slept.

In the morning, I awoke with a strange feeling of unease. My husband, who had slept peacefully through the storm, was looking out the window. He turned to me.

"I'm sorry to tell you," he said. There was a sadness in his eyes. "I'm really sorry, but our big pine tree is down. Uprooted by the wind."

It was true. The 50-foot tree, which had stood proudly in front of our house for all those seasons, would stand no more. Those pine needles, which had shaded us in summer, those branches, which had sheltered cardinals and squirrels and supported our boys in happy climbs higher than the rooftop – this loving tree now lay defeated by its enemy, the wind.

"Isn't it strange?" mused my husband. "A great living thing like that tree can go down without even being able to cry out."

"Not true," I whispered to the stricken tree. "I heard you cry, old friend. I heard you cry."

This appeared in The Columbus Dispatch

Next door neighbors and "BFFs" Dena (the birthday girl, left) and Teddy (right) suffer the humiliation of wearing party hats while patiently waiting for cupcake time to begin.

Victory Gardens

As told to Sandy Whitehead by Wanda Kelly

Wanda Kelly recalls that during World War II everyone was encouraged to have a Victory Garden. Many Westgate residents had cultivated plots for vegetable gardens in an open field where Westgate Elementary School is now located. Wanda remembers many a day, along with a friend, going to hoe the weeds.

Wanda's relatives are from Arkansas and she has three distance cousins by the name of Hodges buried in Camp Chase Confederate Cemetery.

Joyce Rector's pets Tiger (left) and Sugar (right) share a relaxing moment.

Pizza Spaghetti

Submitted by Sally Yocom

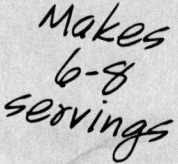
Makes 6-8 servings

----

3 oz. package sliced pepperoni or turkey pepperoni

1 medium onion, chopped

6 oz. uncooked spaghetti, broken in thirds

3-8 oz. cans tomato sauce

6 oz. shredded Swiss cheese (may use low-fat cheese)

½ tsp. oregano

8 oz. shredded mozzarella cheese (may use low-fat cheese)

----

1. In 6-quart cooking pot, boil chopped onion, pepperoni, and broken spaghetti together in 4 quarts of water for 8 minutes.
2. Drain.
3. Rinse with cold water and drain again.
4. In the same pot, stir the remaining ingredients into the spaghetti mixture.
5. Spray a 2-quart casserole dish with non-stick cooking spray.
6. Pour the mixed ingredients into the casserole dish.
7. Cover and place in a casserole dish on a cookie sheet.
8. Preheat oven to 350 and bake for one hour.

The Blue Heron of Westgate

Submitted by Mari Ann Binder Futty

A few years ago, I convinced my husband John to build a pond for our backyard garden. It was great! We had been fairly successful keeping water plants and fish alive (not so much the frogs), so our little habitat was more or less flourishing. And then one morning IT came. John saw a large shadow, and then a pterodactyl-like creature landed on the lawn and headed for the pond. By the time John ran outside, the heron was standing in the pond and had gotten at least one of our fish. My husband went into full-on research mode, searching the internet and quizzing other victimized pond-owners in Westgate on how to best protect our pond from the beast.

Here are his results, from least to most effective (so far):

Placing a screen or netting over the pond: not a good plan, since herons use their claws and beaks to rip right through the covering.

Positioning a fake heron or two by the pond: If you do this, you have to keep moving it/them, since apparently, herons are smart enough to recognize an imposter and detect movement or the lack of it.

Criss-crossing (50 pound weight) fishing line across and running it around the perimeter of the pond: My husband has devised an intricate pattern of fishing line that (according to "experts'), herons can see from the sky and detect as a danger. In addition, John found out that herons like to walk rather than swoop into water, so he ran the line around the pond, about 6 inches off the ground to "trip up" the intruder. He also put a decorative fence on the side of the pond adjacent to the yard, where the heron was most likely to stroll into the water. Finally, we added a few hiding places for the fish – a low, plastic table in the deepest part of the pond and plastic piping (so, like, a little covered patio and a tunnel).

I've told friends and neighbors that if they have any precious jewels or coin collections, they might want to consider storing them in our pond, as my husband's "James Bond" approach to protecting our pond has resulted in a Fort Knox level of security for our fish-family. So far.

Our Menagerie

Submitted by Linda Barnhart Lowry

I had many pets. We had a cat named Tacky; two dogs named Spotty and Scamp; my goldfish and a tank of lots of fancy guppies. I also had a parakeet named Pecky; a rooster named Noodles Senior; a pet squirrel I raised from a baby named Noodles Junior. My rooster was a Leghorn and was very friendly. We took him to relatives on a farm when he started to sing. Think our neighbors had had enough of his singing. I also had a pet squirrel from the time it was a baby. Found him at Westgate Park. Checked on him for several days, his mother never came back to help him. Brought him home and he stayed in the cage Dad and I had built for Noodles Sr. (the rooster). Noodles Jr. lived in the garage in his cage when Dad and I weren't home. We knew when he was ready to be released back to the wild. He came back every day to see us and get his peanuts.

One of Linda Barnhart Lowry's many pets was a rooster named Noodles, Sr.

Tippy the Squirrel

Submitted by Scott Whitehead

I grew up on the first block of S. Huron which was lined with trees, so we had many squirrels. With peanuts and patience I befriended one who I named Tippy. When Tippy began trying to come in the front door, my mom said no more peanuts for the squirrels!

Scott Whitehead learns the price of friendship is peanuts.

My Mother's Garden

Submitted by Lia Eastep

My mother, Phyllis Eastep, has one of the most beautiful yards in Westgate. To say I never fully understood what this meant while I was growing up would be an understatement. I had zero interest in her hobby. Maybe because I didn't see it as a hobby; to me it seemed more like part of one's weekly domestic routine – balance the checkbook, change the sheets, work in the yard.

One night, as an adult, I was standing with my mother in her kitchen, me rinsing dishes for her to put in the dishwasher after a meatloaf meal. I looked out into her backyard and asked her why she did it. She knew what I meant – the hours and hours of tedious clipping, the tugging and planning, the browsing, buying, and constant watering. I expected an understated answer, a modest dismissal even, reducing her passion to the comforts of routine. Instead, she turned off her faucet, gazed out the back window, beyond the top of her contorted filbert, across the grand display of pansies, hostas, little statues and miniature flags. She turned to me and said with great certainty, "Because it's all just so beautiful now isn't it?"

When we moved into our new house on Crescent Drive in 1978, it was my job to pick up twigs out of the front yard before my dad mowed. It was a tedious job I begrudged because I felt there were certainly better ways to be spending my time, like visiting Deb, the sweet and funny pregnant lady across the street. Sometimes my mom would have me help her while she weeded. She would sometimes send me to the garage in search of a specific tool, only to find me ten minutes later on our next door neighbor's porch, a glass of lemonade in my hand and their little dog in my lap.

In 2004, I bought a house on S. Sylvan. One day, Mom gave me a bag of tulip bulbs that I put aside when I got home and forgot about. A few weeks later, on a whim, I planted them into the ground and forgot about them again. When their green tips began peeking out from the earth, I got excited. I checked their progress every single day when I got home, and sometimes even before I went to bed.

Later that summer, Mom said I could take some clippings from her yard. I followed behind her with a bucket of tools while she drove a shovel into the center of her luscious plants. When I made a face in response to the ripping and crunching sound, she reassured me. "It'll be okay. I've taken plenty away from these plants and they always come back." When we transplanted them into my yard they looked limp. My mother assured me that they would bounce back if I watered them regularly. Which I did every day, until they could manage on their own.

I wish I could say that having my mother's plants in my beds sparked a great interest in gardening. Alas, that has not happened. While I may not ever inherit my mother's green thumb, I do embody her intolerance for being idle. Her impulse for consistent maintenance is manifested in my need to read, write and edit;

thousands of musings, reflections, jottings and shaping prose accumulating into a life's work. I think my mother's life's work is her gardening.

This interest extends well beyond her yard. Riding in the car with my mother anywhere can become an impromptu garden tour. She is inclined to point out the beauty in the most unlikely of places – sprouting buds in the cracks along the sidewalk, in a flower bed tucked between a corn dog stand and souvenir booth, in the blanketing of wild lilacs along a grassy highway divide.

The Eastep home on Crescent Drive

Rolled Ginger Cookies
Submitted by Ric Brandel

1 cup Shortening
5 cup Flour
1 cup Sugar
1–½ teaspoons Baking Soda
1 Egg
½ teaspoon Salt
1 cup Molasses
2 to 3 teaspoons Ginger
2 tablespoons Vinegar
1 teaspoons Cinnamon
1 teaspoons Ground Cloves

Cream sugar and shortening, beat in egg, molasses and vinegar

Sift together dry ingredients and blend in

Chill 3 hours

Roll on floured surface ½ inch thick, and cut into shapes

Bake on greased cookie sheet at 375 degrees for 5-6 minutes

The Unseen Overseer

As told to Sandy Whitehead by Allan & Phyllis South

When Allan and Phyllis South purchased their home on Brinker, the upstairs was unfinished. The family who built the home had one child and didn't need the extra bedroom. Phyllis said it reminded her of a church with its peaked ceiling.

After moving in, Allan and Phyllis decided to finish the upstairs. During the time they worked on the second floor 400 sq. feet master suite, Phyllis said she felt a presence. It was as if someone was watching the progress.

In discussing it with others, they thought it was Mary, the first owner of the home. She had come back to watch the second floor of her home being completed. When the project was finished they never felt her presence again.

Our Powhatan Avenue Ghost

Submitted by Melissa Rentko

An oddity about this house is, when I first moved in, there was indeed a ghost or spirit or something, in the smallest bedroom, which until I moved in, was the primary bedroom being used by the previous owner, Mrs. Fagan. For example, my then-boyfriend and I were upstairs painting late one night, and suddenly, clear as day, we heard what sounded like a rubber ball bouncing on the attic floor above us, over and over, and very loud. However, this house's attic has no floor; it was never finished. Therefore, that was pretty impossible. We heard similar sounds over time, as did overnight guests; and once a friend, visiting our home for the first time, stopped dead in her tracks at the doorway of that bedroom, turned pale, and whispered, "There's someone in here." I'd never told her we had an "occupant," because I didn't want to sound crazy! The sounds eventually ceased, and I haven't heard anything more in about 10 years.

The Muffin Ghost of Crescent Drive

Submitted by David and Suzanna Caperton

In late 1993, we learned that Suzanna was expecting. It was an exciting time for our family and the days were soon filled with doctor visits, picking out names and getting our house at the east end of Crescent Drive ready for our family expansion. All the while we were both teaching full time and between house preparations and the regular load of grading papers and planning lessons, by bedtime most evenings we were pretty well ready for a few hours of uninterrupted sleep. But one January night in 1994, I awoke about 3 am to the unmistakable sweet smell of baking muffins. In my half-dream state, I assumed that Suzanna was up and—as she sometimes did—preparing some treat for her students and teacher friends at school. The next night, I was once again coaxed from sleep by the smell of baking and this time I glanced at the clock to see it was not yet 4 o'clock. I turned over and there was Suzanna still asleep beside me. I nudged her awake and asked what she had put in to bake, worried that it might burn if she slept through the timer. "I'm not baking anything," she slurred sleepily. "Then what's that smell?" I asked her. She propped herself up on one elbow and sniffed the air. "It smells like muffins," she said, now sounding fully awake.

We got out of bed and walked downstairs to the kitchen. No smell of baking was evident there and the oven was cold and dark. We theorized that it was either our neighbor Kathy who sometimes surprised us with a coconut pie or a loaf of warm zucchini bread or the Big Bear store that was still in the old tan block building at Broad and Hague that was somehow sending the good smells our way. How the aroma from anywhere was getting into just our bedroom in January — when we had every door and window tightly shut — was just part of the mystery. Over the next few weeks, we awoke several more times in the hours between 2 and 5 am to the delicious smells of baking muffins. Finally, we asked our neighbor, if she had taken to baking late at night, and she laughed and said, no, she cooked and baked only during the daylight hours. We asked next at the bakery at Big Bear, and they also told us that they had no bakers or oven going before 5 am.

We began to refer to the phenomenon as the work of our "Muffin Ghost." Although it was a little unnerving to wake to smells of baking with no good explanation, we never felt afraid. The Muffin Ghost visits got to be something we kind of liked. It was sort of like being haunted by the ghost of Aunt Bea.

Once Alex was born, we had fewer visitations by the Muffin Ghost, but it still came around from time to time. Once, when Alex was two or three, he called to us from his bedroom about 3 in the morning and asked if he could have some of the chocolate chip cookies he smelled. We stumbled into his room to tell him he had just dreamed them, but when we got into the room, the smell was undeniable (and we wanted some too).

Now the Muffin Ghost makes only occasional visits, but it has expanded its menu from just muffins or cookies and has awoken us with the smells of toast, bacon and even coffee (its specialty is apparently breakfast). Our only complaint about our paranormal pastry chef is that just once we'd like a manifestation that we could taste as well as smell.

Hauntingly Good Plum Muffins
(So good it's spooky)

2 cups self-rising flour

2 cups sugar

1 cup crushed almonds (optional)

2 teaspoons allspice

3 eggs

1 cup oil

2 small jars of baby food plums

Preheat oven to 325 degrees. Combine all ingredients and mix thoroughly. Pour into miniature muffin tins and bake for approximately 15 minutes.

The Snow Ghost

Submitted by Suzanna Caperton

I have only shared the pie recipe with my sister since many of my students (and even some staff members) believed in the legend. If it's shared with too many people, it loses its magic. I came across the recipe as a teen while waiting for an appointment. The magazines in the office were years out of date, and I was flipping through them disinterestedly when the words "snow ghost" caught my eye. I should be ashamed to say that I tore the article and recipe out of the magazine, but it was so obviously unwanted that I felt it was a rescue.

The legend is of a Snow Ghost who, under the right weather conditions, will accept a piece of chocolate pie. If this happens, school will be closed for snow at least one day. I shared this tale with my students over 31 years. The newcomers always begin with doubt, but veteran students swear that it works. I promised them I would always have the ingredients at the ready so if the conditions were right, I could create an offering for the ghost.

Over the years I received many evening calls from students and staff asking if the time was right for the pie. I can't remember a time it failed us. About 20 years ago the conditions were right. The calls began early and came from students and staff. Even a few teachers at the high school where David, my husband taught, called. I began the process and David laughed. I baked through his teasing and left a piece for the Snow Ghost.

The next morning the only school in Central Ohio not closed for snow was his district. When he finally skidded to school (2 hours late), his friends asked why I didn't make the pie. He had to grudgingly admit that I made it, but the Snow Ghost didn't appreciate his lack of belief.

Snow Ghost Pie

1 baked pie crust	1/2 cup cocoa	1-1/4 cups sugar
1/3 cup cornstarch	1/4 teaspoon salt	3 tablespoons butter
3 cups milk	1-1/2 tsp. vanilla	Sweetened whipped cream

Combine cocoa, sugar, salt, and cornstarch in a medium saucepan. Gradually blend milk into dry ingredients, stirring until smooth. (A whisk works best.) Cook over medium heat, stirring constantly, until filling boils; boil 1 minute. Remove from heat; blend in butter and vanilla. Pour into crust. Cover with plastic wrap. Cool; chill 3-4 hours. Garnish with whipped cream. I decorate each piece with snow flake dollops of whipped cream, or marshmallow ghosts.

Each Halloween, trick-or-treaters anxiously approach the house occupied by the Capertons and their Muffin Ghost. Above: The "theme" conjured up by Dave, Suzanna and Alex for Halloween 2012, "Once Upon A Time," was perfect for the Tudor-style house, which they decorated to look like a Grimm's Fairy Tale cottage.

Ghost of 2937 Fremont Street

Submitted by Lou & Sandy Whitehead

Perhaps those of you who grew up in the area remember going to the Ritz, Rivali or downtown Dreamland theaters. George Pekras owned all three. Josephine Pekras, George's wife, purchased the 2937 Fremont lot in 1941. Previously, Henry Binns had purchased it in 1924, Willie Herd and Henry Holton in 1928, eventually selling it in 1937 to Hasle and Ruth Herd.

Building began on a one-story brick home in 1941. However, while residing in a motel someone tried to break into their room and Mrs. Pekras declared once she moved from that motel, she would never again sleep in a room located on a ground floor. The plans for a one-story home changed to the present two-story. It is alleged George visited each day to keep track of the building process. The Pekras' were devoted Roman Catholics who attended St. Mary Magdalene Church. Metals of the gospels are in each corner stone and above the living room fireplace were three marble insets placed for statues of the Sacred Heart and two others. In the entrance hallway was Josephine's kneeler for daily prayers and a priest came each month to bless the home. Sometime during the 1950's, George passed away, at home, but continues to live here (in spirit!). Josephine lived in the home until 1981, moving to a nursing home at the age of 90.

We purchased the home in January 1982. Josephine died one month later. Before moving, Lou was working in the basement. There was a heavy sound of footsteps on the first floor. Finding no one there, doors locked, windows closed, and although not being a person easily spooked, he quickly left.

Soon we began smelling a strong odor of Cherry Blend pipe tobacco of which George smoked. There is a cedar closet located at the top of the stairs leading to the second floor. Although being shut tightly it would often be ajar. I like the smell of Cherry Blend but several months after moving in, I decided to have a chat with George. One day when the door had become ajar and I smelled pipe tobacco, I sat at the top of the stairs and had that chat. I told George how much we loved his house. Any updates were only to make it a comfortable home for our family and hoped he would approve of any changes.

During the year's we have lived in the home George returns only when we have been making some change. He no longer returns when we redecorate such as painting but does return when we do any major work. The latest was when we installed new windows.

The yearly haunting of Binns Island is a hair-raising sight when dozens of ghosts, goblins, critters and creatures emerge from the shadows on the Sunday before Halloween.

Top: At the Hilltop Historical Society's annual memorial service at Camp Chase Cemetery, some women come dressed as Louisiana Ransburgh Briggs may have done when she secretly laid flowers at the graves of Confederate soldiers in the years following the Civil War.

Bottom: The grave of the soldier who was the inspiration for one of the ghost stories of Camp Chase Cemetery.

The Veiled Lady of Camp Chase

Submitted by Mari Ann Binder Futty

Dick Hoffman also contributed to this piece

There are certainly tales and legends about Camp Chase Cemetery – the most famous are about a woman identified as *"The Lady in Gray"* or *"The Veiled Lady."* It doesn't take much digging to find stories of a woman who wanders through the cemetery weeping, searching for her betrothed among the headstones. (Some stories identify the subject of the ghost's search as Benjamin Allen, a soldier from Tennessee.) Other legends identify a veiled lady who leaves flowers at the graves of the soldiers, or specifically at Benjamin Allen's grave.

At least some bits and pieces of these stories are based on a woman who actually lived. Louisiana Ransburgh Briggs was a Southern sympathizer who came north with her husband a few years after the Civil War ended and lived near the site of Camp Chase. Surrounded by Northerners, many of whom were either Union veterans or had lost family members in the war (some in Confederate prisons), Mrs. Briggs paid her respects to the Confederate dead in secret, usually at night and always hiding her identity by wearing a heavy veil. As the years passed, she faithfully carried flowers to the cemetery, and in 1917 at a reunion of the United Confederate Veterans she was honored as the "Confederate Angel of Camp Chase."

Louisiana Ransburgh Briggs

Who knows? A ghost or two may be hovering about the cemetery. After all, it's true that there was a "Veiled Lady" who visited the graves. It's also true that cemeteries abound with ghost stories; and as cemeteries go, there can be no more sorrowful place than one where young men died so tragically, and so far from home.

Block Parties

Submitted by Sandy Whitehead

Between 1966 and 1982, our family resided at 42 South Huron Ave. That strip of South Huron begins at West Broad Street and ends at Crescent Dr. Not being a through street, it was one with very little traffic. The neighbors found the street to be great for block parties. We all enjoyed getting together to eat while we visited and the children played games.

Moving to 2937 Fremont St. our family again enjoyed a Block party on our street but on a much larger scale. On September 18, 1999, the Camp Chase Blockwatch hosted a big block party in front of our home.

Police closed the streets of Fremont Street between Roys Ave. and Binns Blvd. plus Fremont to the alley at Guernsey. Neighbors enjoyed an afternoon and evening of food and activities. Not pictured is a Columbus Fire Department hook and ladder truck as well as the Mounted Police Unit. Fearless neighbors enjoyed a ride to great heights in the bucket.

Goldfish Make Bad Party Favors

Submitted by Matt Jaynes

I have so many memories of growing up in Westgate. Before the age of video and computer games we spent most of our time playing outside. There were so many kids my own age that it was never hard to find something to do. It could have been simply tossing a football or a game of pickup basketball next door. In the winter we would all bundle up and make snowmen or snow forts in our front yards.

My birthday parties always had a theme. One year it was a fish theme and all the boys were sent home with a live gold fish. I've got to say my mother was not very popular with the other mothers that year and was made to promise not to have a puppy theme party in the future!!

But it was my 6th birthday that was my favorite. My dad painted a football field in our back yard – complete with yard lines, MATT FIELD and goal posts. It was the perfect way to wear out a bunch of 6-year old boys before allowing them to sleep over.

Even though most of us have since moved away we remain great friends to this day. Growing up in Westgate in the 80s was a great experience.

My very own field!

S'MEEPS
Submitted by Sandy Whitehead

Linda Barnhart Lowry and her family pose in their Easter finery in this 1950s snapshot.

This recipe puts a colorful spring spin on the traditional S'mores

- Graham crackers
- Hershey chocolate bars
- Peeps, Chicks, or bunnies, you decide

1. Place a square of chocolate on a graham cracker
2. Top with your choice of Peep.
3. Place on a plate and zap in the microwave for just a few seconds or until softened.

Halloween Costumes a Scream!

Submitted by Beth Chamberlin & Kathy Seibert

Kathy and I have lived together in Westgate for nearly 15 years. She actually has lived here for 18 years but the time before I came into the picture doesn't count (at least not in my mind).

One of our favorite times of the year is Halloween. We especially look forward to Beggars' Night and we usually wear some type of costumes while we hand out candy. Kathy has a perverse need to try and scare everyone that she can!

We enjoy seeing all of the cute and scary costumes. There have been some great homemade costumes such as the hand sewn Sherlock Holmes, Legos out of a cardboard box, and the foam candy corn piece.

Then there are also the not-so-creative costumes; we all know that when you live in Columbus, wearing an OSU jersey does NOT count as a costume!

The diversity of our neighborhood is also reflected in the kids' outfits. One year there was a hilarious cross-dressing couple.

He was especially funny in a skirt, wig, and make-up, trying to walk in heels! There was once a "lesbian couple" holding hands & wearing flannel shirts. Hello? Can you say stereotypes?? It's fun to ask what they're supposed to be so they can explain.

A few years back we even had a celebrity stop by for Trick or Treat. That's right, our own Mayor Michael Coleman. I guess he stops somewhere in Westgate every year on Beggars' Night and passes out candy. He was kind enough to pose for a picture with me in my green M&M costume.

We have also learned a few things over the years. Kathy has learned that she can't pass out candy wearing a scary clown mask; it makes little kids cry!

We have also learned that kids don't care what the weather is. If you're giving out free candy, they will be there to get it!

One thing we haven't seemed to learn is how much candy to buy. Every year, we just about double the amount of candy from the year before, and every year we run out after only an hour. In 2012 – when it was a damp 39° we went through 450 pieces in 50 minutes giving out only 1 piece per person!

Next year I'm aiming for 1,000 pieces. Maybe that will be the year we won't have to turn out our light before Trick or Treat is over.

HOLIDAY BEAN CASSEROLE

Submitted by Deborah Dahlen Buzard

1 bag Fordhook lima beans

1 bag cut green beans

1 pound fresh mushrooms, sliced

1 pt. container whipping cream (do not whip)

My mother, Shirley Kietzman Dahlen, made this casserole every Christmas. I make it for my brothers and myself every holiday.

The night before cook beans together – but do not overcook – as you will be baking them in the oven.

Sauté mushrooms in butter. Add cooked beans to mushrooms and pour whipping cream over mixture. Refrigerate overnight.

The next day allow the casserole to come to room temperature while preheating your oven to 350°. Bake until bubbly and heated through.

Recipe can be adjusted to amount that you need to serve.

At Christmastime in the 1950s, Santa Claus arrived at Westgate Park on an ornate float.

Holidays in Westgate

Submitted by Elizabeth Hylton

At Halloween, Beggars Night was quite an event on our street and the street would be filled with many children. At one house, the owner placed plastic pumpkins on each of his lights at his front door. When you rang the doorbell a recorded voice announced that they were the great pumpkin (high tech in those days) and wished you a Happy Halloween before the door opened and you were given your treats. As children, we really believed those pumpkins were speaking to us. Usual treats were candy, apples, popcorn balls, pennies and, the ultimate treat, candy bars. One neighbor gave flavored paraffin shaped as women's lips that were brightly colored and paraffin bottles filled with a flavored drink. She always presented a tray of these items and would let us choose what we wanted.

At Christmastime our streets would be really decorated. Two homes on my street always stood out. Our neighbors, who lived directly across the street from us, had a large bay window in which they would place a huge beautifully decorated Christmas tree. I loved seeing their tree and wanted to have a Christmas tree just like theirs. On Christmas Eve they would place a life sized cardboard figure of Santa Claus on their porch. It resembled some of the old Santas that one sees on Coca-Cola advertisements. My siblings and I were so excited when they placed the Santa on their porch because we knew that Santa would be visiting us that evening.

A family who lived at the corner of Wicklow Road and South Southampton had Christmas lights all over their property. They also had many decorated Christmas trees in their windows. One tree might be done in all blue while another in all orange. Several large pine trees bordered the back of their property and those trees would be strung with Christmas lights. Later the family topped those trees and sold the tops as Christmas trees. Our family purchased one of those tree tops and it was probably the largest tree we ever had. Years later when the family had passed away and their household items were sold, I was able to purchase a lovely ornament from their collection. Every year when I hang that ornament, I think of their family and remember how much they enjoyed decorating for the Christmas season.

Happy Birthday, 106 Binns Boulevard!

Submitted by John and Mari Ann Futty

In the summer of 2010, my husband and I threw a 70th birthday party for … our house! We tried to bring as much of the era as we could to the celebration.

The props: We had movie posters of films that premiered that year: "The Grapes of Wrath" and "Rebecca" (which was showing on one of our televisions during the party); a 1940 newsreel looped on another TV; copies of books that were published that year were on display: Native Son and For Whom The Bell Tolls; and a CD of songs that were popular in 1940, including "In The Mood," "All The Things You Are," "I'll Never Smile Again," and "When You Wish Upon A Star," played on the stereo.

The refreshments: While we didn't recreate an exact menu from the era (no jellied aspic!), we did have items that would have been found at either a casual supper party or barbeque, including baked ham, potato salad, and an extensive "relish tray." I did serve potato chips, but I think our party was the only one in the past decade where there were no tortilla chips or salsa on the

Popcorn Cake

1 Pound (64 Large) Marshmallows
1 Stick Butter
¼ Cup Oil
12 Cups Popped Popcorn
2 Cups M&Ms
1 Cup Cocktail Peanuts

Submitted by
Mari Ann Binder Tutty

✦✦✦✦✦
This recipe is great for kids to help with!
✦✦✦✦✦

1. Oil or spray a bundt cake pan with non-stick cooking spray.
2. Melt together in a saucepan or in the microwave: marshmallows, butter, and oil. Allow this mixture to cool slightly (so the M&Ms don't melt) before pouring it over the popcorn, M&Ms and cocktail peanuts.
   Variation: Substitute candy corn for the M&Ms at Halloween time.
3. Press mixture into the bundt pan, and allow to set-up for at least two hours before turning out onto a cake plate. *Slicing should be done by a grown-up, as a sharp knife is needed.*

buffet! My research showed that wine was not part of the offerings at parties in 1940, so the alcohol was limited to Schlitz beer, hard alcohol with old-style mixers (club soda, ginger ale and tonic), and gin martinis with olives and cocktail onions. We even managed to find some Frosty Orange Soda and Dad's Root Beer for the occasion. Although we did use paper napkins, we broke out the silver, crystal and china, as would have been done for party guests in 1940 – no paper plates or plastic ware for this party!

The clothes: I think our favorite part of the party was that so many of our friends and neighbors dressed in vintage clothing, donned hats, spectator shoes and some even got the look down to the details of rhinestone jewelry, seamed stockings, wide neckties or suspenders. (One neighbor who attended our party was a volunteer at our house a year later for the Westgate Home & Garden Tour, and dressed in her 1940s attire as she guided tour guests through our house!)

Kentucky Benedictine Dip

Submitted by Mari Ann Binder Futty

I made this appetizer for the Westgate Derby Day Dash in 2010. It was served at the house that featured dishes traditionally served at the Kentucky Derby, including "Kentucky Hot Browns."

~ 1 large cucumber, pared, shredded and drained
~ 1 tablespoon mayonnaise
~ 8 ounces softened cream cheese
~ 1 tablespoon sour cream
~ 2 tablespoons grated onion
~ Dash of green food coloring

Combine all ingredients. Serve with crackers, pita chips or raw veggies.

Maddox Wedding Reception

Submitted by Sandy and Lou Whitehead

On June 4, 1988 the backyard of our home at 2937 Fremont St. was the wedding reception venue for daughter Debbie and her new husband, Shawn. Large white tents protected the round tables covered with flowers. The back porch was transformed into the catering line complete with bar and bartender. The weather was absolutely perfect and the beautiful back yard provided a backdrop for lots of pictures.

The day after the Maddox wedding we hosted an outdoor breakfast for relatives and close friends. Immediately following breakfast the pink bows and wedding décor came down, and up went Bishop Ready colors of blue and white plus congratulations signs for our son Scott's high school graduation party held later that day.

It was one of our busier weekends, to say the least!

Our new son-in-law Shawn learned on his wedding day that he had married into a family that loved to play practical jokes. His new uncle had locked the door to the room where their honeymoon clothes were, so Shawn had to climb through a window to retrieve them.

The Perfect Wedding

Submitted by Kelly McKinney

In 2005, Mary and I in invited 60 of our closest friends and family to our new home for a house warming party with a "surprise at 5 pm." Each guest was asked to bring a favorite food/dish with recipe to share... What a great time!!

At 5 pm after the feast, while friends and family were relaxing in the "pristine, perfect October day in Westgate," Mary and I included all of them in an unannounced but perfectly planned stress-free wedding! In 2012 we celebrated our 7-year wedding anniversary with love and gratitude.

1986 Easter Egg Hunt in Westgate Park.

Pumpkin Pie C*A*K*E

Submitted by Charlotte Ogden

Bake at 350 for 1 hour and 15 minutes.

Serve warm with whipped cream or topping.

CRUST

1 box (2 layer) yellow cake mix (reserve 1 cup for topping)
½ c (1 stick) margarine (very soft)
1 egg

Mix ingredients and press into a 9x13-inch pan.

FILLING

1 large (1lb. 13oz.) can pumpkin
2 tsp. cinnamon
3 eggs
1 c. sugar
2/3 c. evaporated milk

Mix ingredients together and pour over crust.

TOPPING

1 c. reserved cake mix
¼ c. margarine, softened
½ c. sugar
1 c. pecans, chopped

Mix reserved cake mix, sugar and margarine together until crumbly. Sprinkle over filling. Sprinkle pecans on top.

Our Backyard Easter Egg Hunt

Submitted by Jerry and Betty Jaynes

Over 30 years ago, as newlyweds, we were renting in Grandview. We looked at numerous homes in Grandview but stumbled on Westgate where we found similar style homes. With interest rates topping 18%...that is not a typo... we felt lucky to have found a homeowner who was willing to finance us at 10%. Hard to believe with today's rates that we thought 10% was a bargain!!

We moved into our new home and were greeted by neighbors who had lived in Westgate for decades having raised their families. By the time we started our family many other young families moved in. Within a few years there were over 40 kids within a half a block.

When the kids were very young I organized an Easter Egg hunt – with our backyard hosting the 5 &6 year olds, our neighbor hosting the 3 & 4 year olds and yet another hosting the 1 & 2 year olds. This picture shows just a few of the dozens of children getting ready for the hunt in 1989.

As the kids grew, many summer nights were spent playing hide-and-seek, dodge ball or just catching fireflies.

Now, as many of the neighbors who welcomed us have moved to retirement homes or have passed away, we find that we are the empty nesters welcoming new young families. And so the neighborhood is once again filled with the squeals of little ones.

We still love our neighborhood, and love seeing the revitalization of the West Broad corridor.

Parrothead Patio Party

Submitted by Bob Waddell and Patti Von Niessen

We moved into the neighborhood in July of 2009 and each year since then, we've thrown the Parrothead Patio Party as our featured Westgate Night Out. This is our way of giving back to a neighborhood that's been so welcoming to us since we arrived. We felt embraced as part of a unique, tight-knit community and quickly had many good friends and acquaintances. To us, Westgate feels more like a small village, than part of a large anonymous city. If you've lived in Westgate for any length of time, you'll know what we mean. If you're new to Westgate, well, you just need to mark your calendar for July's Westgate Night Out and come and meet the neighborhood at the Parrothead Patio Party where you'll be adorned with a welcoming lei, offered a straw hat, and have a margarita or glass of sangria placed in your hand.

Steve's Ultimate Pasta
Submitted by Patti Von Niessen

2 Cups Pasta (Tortellini or other)

1 8 oz. Jar Pesto Sauce or Homemade

1 Small Jar Oil Soaked Sundried Tomatoes (sliced)

1 Small Jar Artichoke Hearts

Mushrooms (sliced and sautéed)

Green Onions

Red or Orange Bell Pepper (chopped fine)

Fresh Spinach (big handful)

1 Small Package Smoked Salmon (slivered)

1. Cook Pasta.

2. Drain and Add Sun Dried Tomatoes Plus Their Oil, and Remaining Ingredients

3. If Pasta is a Bit Dry, Add Some Liquid from the Jar of Artichoke Hearts

These Wonderful Westgate Homes

Submitted by Betty Jaynes

Older homes speak to you...with charm, character and soul. Newer homes lack something intangible...they just don't hit you in the heart.

When looking for a first home, many people are drawn to Westgate. While newer developments might have more modern conveniences, newer homes lack roots and emotional appeal.

Ask Westgate residents what drew them to the area and most will say the historic charm and affordability of the homes.

Once here they will tell you the neighborhood is more than just a collection of homes built in the 20's, 30's and 40's. They will tell you that it has been like stepping back in time – where neighbors care about one another – and actually know one another.

Westgate – not just a neighborhood – a way of life. But let's allow our fellow residents to say for themselves what drew them here, or how the neighborhood has touched them.

Charming, in a Drippy Sort of Way

Submitted by Tom Prince and Ron Koziol

Tom and I moved to Westgate in the mid 80's. I loved the area and the older homes. But with the character and charm often comes repairs.

The previous owners mentioned that the roof had leaked, but it had been repaired. It was only after the first hard rain that I found out what their idea of repair was.

I noticed dampness on the ceiling and after removing the damaged ceiling I discovered 3 large dish pans – one of which fell, soaking me. I can only assume they thought the pans would catch the rain and then evaporate before the next storm.

The roof has since been properly repaired so now rains are welcomed for Tom's extensive perennial and mum gardens.

Mary Frances Prince's Raisin-Filled Cookie Recipe

Submitted by Tom Prince

This holiday cookie recipe was passed down from my grandmother, Annie Eiler, to my mother, Mary Frances Prince. My grandparents, Henry & Annie Eiler (on my mom's side of the family) lived in Dover, Ohio, and were candy makers for over 50 years. The Eiler Candy Shop, known for its homemade chocolates and candies still exists today in downtown Dover. My cousin, John Gibbs, now operates the candy business.

Dough

2 eggs
1 cup margarine (or lard)
7 cups flour
2 teaspoons baking soda
2 cups sugar
1 cup milk
4 teaspoons cream of tartar
2 teaspoons vanilla extract

Sift all dry ingredients (except sugar) together in a separate bowl. Cream margarine and sugar until fluffy; add eggs and vanilla until well combined. Gradually add sifted dry ingredients alternately with milk, and mix thoroughly.

Filling

2 cups ground raisins (use meat grinder or food processor)

2 cups sugar   2 cups water   ½-cup flour

Bring ground raisins, sugar, and water to a boil until it thickens. Stir occasionally. Let stand until cool.

Stir in the ½-cup flour, and refrigerate until cold.

Mixture should be thick.

Assembly

Roll out dough thinly (1/8 inch) and cut round pieces with cookie cutter/crimper. Roll out each dough round further, so each round extends beyond the width of crimper. On bottom dough round, place one heaping tablespoon (or more) of cool raisin filling in center of each round, cover with top dough round and crimp with cutter/ crimper. Cookie should look "mounded." Sprinkle top round with Christmas-colored sugar (red or green) and place on greased cookie sheet.

Bake at 350 degrees until golden brown around edges. Best served with milk. Also, best consumed within 24 to 48 hours of baking, as raisin filling will "bleed" into the cookie dough round over time, and cookie integrity will be compromised.

Our Special House

Submitted by Greg and Tasha Corson

Greg and I first moved to Roys Avenue in 1989, shortly after we were married. I soon became involved in the Hilltop Civic Council and founded the Camp Chase Block Watch.

We had always admired a house on Fremont. When it came on the market I was determined to be the highest bidder. I convinced the owner to take the sign out of his yard while we negotiated a final agreement.

While all the homes in Westgate are unique, we like to think ours is pretty special. It is one of the few all-stone homes in the area. It still has 80% of the original leaded glass windows, the original slate roof and copper flashing.

We loved our new neighbors and particularly liked the annual Fremont Block Parties. They got so big we finally had to move them to the schoolyard.

I enjoy raising banana trees in my back yard – carefully moving them to our basement before the first frost.

From the monthly Westgate Nights Out to Boo on Binns to the monthly Euchre Club, we continue to stay involved. Westgate is more than just a collection of houses ... it is our home!

Title of Property Dates to 1794

Submitted by Melissa Rentko

Our house was built in 1935, and as I understand it from the realtor, was a Sears Kit Home, built by the original owners, the Fagans. I can believe they built it themselves, because no room is "square," and in fact, in a couple rooms, the doorway trim was shaved back / truncated because they ran out of wall space! This house also has that useful old laundry chute...except ours is placed directly over a commode in the basement. Hilarious, not to mention completely illogical!

I'm not sure when Mr. Henry Fagan died, but, his wife Mary lived into her 90s. After she went into a nursing home, her children put the house up for sale and about a year later in January 1991, I bought it. I never dreamed I'd live here so long!! I'd intended to stay just 5 years, but it grew on me, and I have such wonderful neighbors.

When I bought this house I received an Abstract of Title that shows the deeds / transfers relating to this property and surrounding area dating back to 1794. I found it all truly fascinating reading. In this Abstract, you can also see names like "Galloway" and "Sullivant." In addition, you can see interesting things like the fact that in 1832, land here was going for $3 per acre. It also shows racism in full swing, as shown by some text from 1932: "No sale shall be made to persons of the colored race, nor to associations or organizations composed of such people. No colored person shall occupy said premises except as a servant." Can you believe that! Oh, my.

The House on Farm Lot #9

Submitted by Joanne Horn Hylton

The house at 182 Powhatan Avenue, currently owned by the Kenneth Helmick family, has had an interesting history. The brick ranch, possibly one of Westgate's first, was built on land originally part of a subdivision surveyed and platted for Michael Sullivant, son and heir of Lucas Sullivant. The subdivision encompasses all of present-day Westgate. Farm lot 9 on which the house at 182 was built passed through a series of owners until Quaker John Cowgill bought the farm after the Civil War. In the early 1900s, the Friends Foreign Missionary Society of the Ohio Yearly Meeting offered for sale that part of the property which they had inherited. These facts are on the abstract currently in the possession of Kenneth Helmick. As the Westgate subdivision developed, the lot and a half remained vacant until Marjorie and Thomas McMillin purchased the lot after World War II. According to a co-worker and neighbor, Marjorie was an excellent typesetter for *The Columbus Dispatch*. Thomas was a heating and cooling specialist.

The McMillans may have been Westgate's first DIYers. They both built the house from footer to roof. Marjorie was seen laying concrete block and brick side by side with Thomas. Except for a bit of updating, the house essentially remains much as it was when built.

Westgate Through a Realtor's Eye

Submitted by Greg and Kelli Watson

As a realtor I have probably been in 60% of the homes in Westgate. Each has a unique character and charm. While many of the homes had similar floor plans when built, over the years each subsequent homeowner has added their own unique upgrades.

I still see the 1960s paneling in basements, occasionally will see avocado green shag carpet in a spare bedroom, and certainly have seen my share of pink bathrooms.

But I also see some spectacular kitchen remodels and back yard living spaces that would be worthy of a layout in *Better Homes & Gardens*.

As I show young families homes in Westgate they are impressed with the features that you just don't find in a newly built track home.

After moving in they soon realize that Westgate has much more to offer than gumwood wood work and interesting built-ins. They soon have neighbors welcoming them and quickly feel a true sense of community.

When Kelli and I got married we moved into my home on Powhatan. We had our first child in November of 2012 and we will likely meet even more of neighbors as we stroll through the park with our new son, Cohen.

PARMESAN CHICKEN BREASTS

Submitted by Jerry Sexton

4 boneless, skinless chicken breasts

¼ cup dry Vermouth

½ cup Parmesan cheese

½ cup flour

3 tbsp. butter

1. Dredge chicken breasts, rinsed and patted dry, in Parmesan cheese patting the cheese into the flesh and lightly shaking off excess.

2. In a non-stick skillet, just large enough to hold chicken without crowding, heat butter until foam begins to subside.

3. Sauté the chicken over moderately high heat until golden brown on each side.

4. Transfer chicken to baking dish, pour vermouth over it and sprinkle with Parmesan cheese.

5. Bake covered loosely in a preheated oven at 325 for 15 minutes.

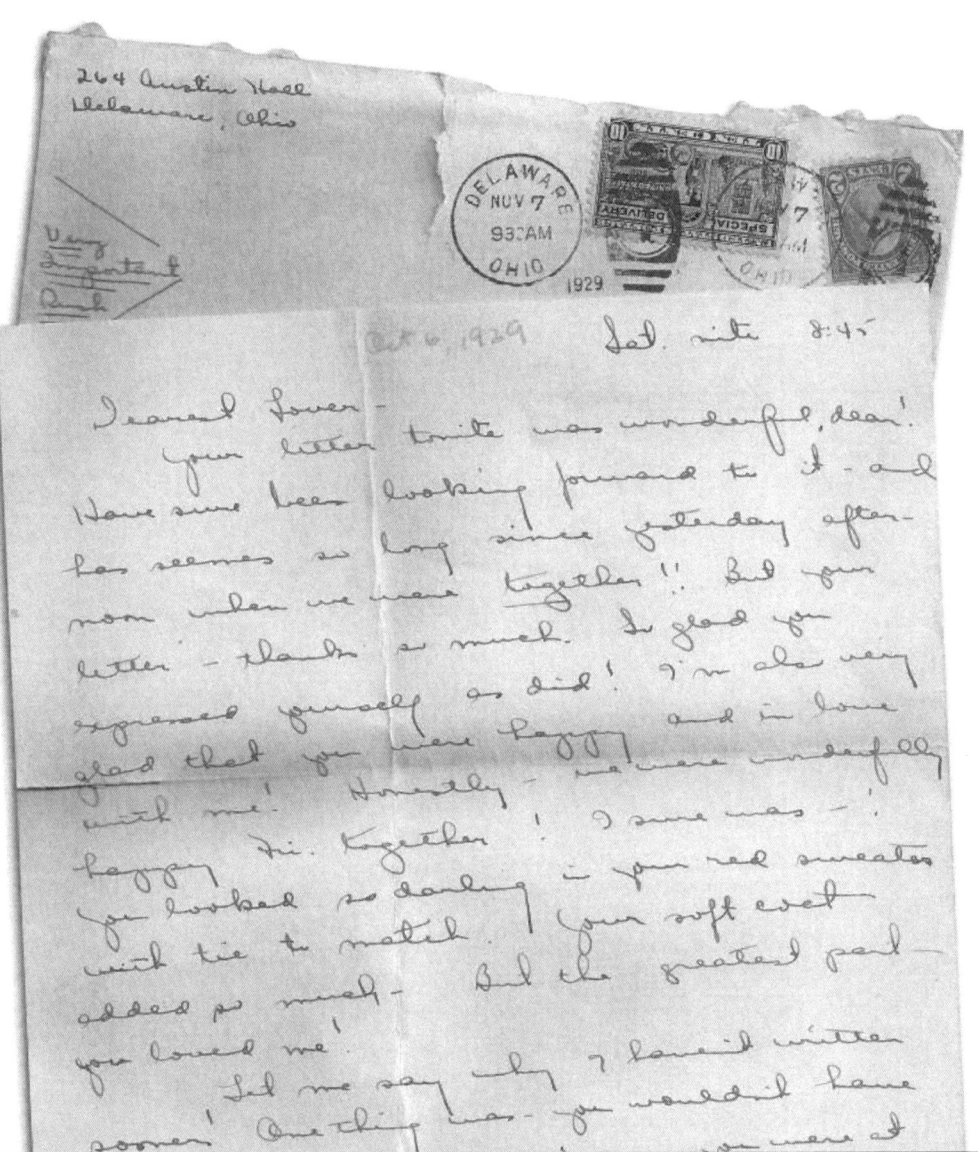

Old houses speak to us in many ways ~
through architectural details, records of past owners, items left behind in the attic or garage, even layers of wallpaper speak of old styles and the personal tastes of former occupants. Jerry Sexton's house on Westgate Avenue did more than speak of times gone by; it told a love story through letters written in 1929 by previous owners of the home. The content of the letters? Well, Jerry considers that private ... his home's own special secret that is not his to tell.

Diet Coke, Chicken Salad & A New Friend

Submitted by Barb Collins

Back in July 1988, my real estate agent and I began the process of finding a home that I could afford. Eventually I would raise my two beautiful daughters, Lindsey and Ashley who I'm very proud of, in this very home. After looking at many houses we came upon the house that I currently live in. I fell in love with it and the neighborhood instantly. I was in the kitchen on my hands and knees scrubbing the floor before we moved in when I heard a knock on my front door. I went to the door, all dirty and sweaty, and when I opened the door I was greeted with a smile from my new neighbor and soon to be good friend with a plate of chicken salad and a diet coke. She (Diane Lazor) said "Welcome, neighbor." We chatted a bit and then she turned and went back home. Later after I moved in we found out we had a lot in common and it was a huge relief knowing she was there. Years have passed and she and her now-husband Greg, have moved, but I still feel very fortunate that I found my house in Westgate and formed a lasting friendship.

The Columbus Evening Dispatch, Sunday, June 15, 1924.

The Barnes home was located on the south side of West Broad Street near Letchworth Avenue.

Edwin P. Barnes Home

Submitted by Joanne Horn Hylton

Edwin Barnes and his family of 5 moved to what is now Westgate about 1918. Mr. Barnes left Cleveland with the promise that his family would be housed in a brick home with a large veranda.

In Cleveland, Edwin P. Barnes was described as a supervisor in a wire shop for a telephone and telegraph company. I suspect this was the Postal Telegraph since my father, who worked for "Postal" was acquainted with Mr. Barnes professionally.

When the Barnes family arrived, they discovered their new home had no porch and the living room contained a switchboard which was used to test lines. The 1919 Columbus City directory identifies Mr. Barnes as "switchboard man" and the house was described as "house ss West Broad 1 e of Big Four RR." The house would have been located somewhere near Letchworth Avenue. A granddaughter who provided pictures and Barnes family history said the station was used to test international lines and the first intercontinental phone call was heard in this office. The large Italianate home was possibility built on the Miller-Gibson farm and was part of the Camp Chase community which existed in this area until absorbed by Columbus. "According to the 1920 census, the western boundary of Columbus was Hague Avenue." Camp Chase was surrounded by farms which appear in pictures in the possession of the Barnes decedents. Doris Barnes Fledderjohann, a daughter of Edwin and Christina, graduated from the old West High School, now Starling Middle School. She recalled the building of the viaduct over West Broad St. which was almost in her front yard. The Barnes family moved from that property about 1925.

Top: Edwin P. Barnes played in the Hilltop band in the early 1920s.

Middle: West Broad Street between 1919 and 1925.

Bottom: The "Camp Chase Community" existed along West Broad Street prior to 1925. Pictured here is one of the Camp Chase cottages.

Three Mothers Remember

Submitted by Betsy Valko, Linda Virden & Sandy Whitehead

During the late 60s through the early 80s, friends Betsy Valko, Linda Virden and Sandy Whitehead enjoyed many hours solving the problems of raising children and enjoyed watching the children race up and down the sidewalk on their trikes and big wheels. Between the three families there were 8 children who were growing up together on a safe street. The sidewalk, beginning at 3003 W. Broad St. and ending at 42 S. Huron Ave., was the pathway between the homes. The older children were responsible for walking the younger children back and forth to school, even at lunch time. They all played outside no matter the season and the three mothers took turns babysitting. Neighbors on S. Huron sat on their porches and visited with each other and when someone was in need of help, someone was there.

Dr. Dick Valko and his wife Betsy purchased 3003 W. Broad St., a residence with a medical office attached, in 1962. Daughters Jenny, Laurie and Valerie grew up in the home. Two unique things about the home are that it has a pink marble fireplace and a three car garage with a car wash. For many years, West High School parade floats were built in the extra large garage!

When moving to Westgate Betsy was impressed with the number and variety of businesses that were present in the area. Haney's Drug Store, the Big Bear Market, a FULL service gas station at the corner of S. Roys and W. Broad, an IGA grocery store and Lawson Dairy practically across the street from their medical office and home at the corner of S. Huron and W. Broad. East of them, on W. Broad St., was a real estate office, a dentist office, a lawyer's office and the Hilltop Library. The Big Bear store had a basement with a pharmacy and a general department store. A one-stop place to get your groceries, medicine, towels, thread, yarn, oil for your car, belts for vacuum cleaners, clothes, household items and many other "goodies." Betsy still resides in the home.

Linda Virden's family moved to Westgate in 1954 to a home on Westgate Ave. After school, she recalls hanging out at the Broadmore Restaurant, located at the corner of Westgate Ave. and W. Broad St. The family shopped at Timlin's IGA grocery and purchased records at the record store on the corner of N. Chase and W. Broad before it became a car-painting garage. Gene Raiser was the disk jockey at the dances held in the enclosed shelter house at Westgate Park. Linda remembers very well the time her sister fell through the ice while ice skating and their dad carried her home. Her grandmother's brother, Curtis Bender, was the first Hilltop soldier killed during WW I.

Pitt & Margaret Knight purchased the lot at 36 S. Huron in December 1925 and built a house during 1926. Mrs. Knight passed away in December 1968 and Don, Linda, Pat, Scott and Cheri Virden moved in during May 1968. Linda still lives in the home.

In April 1966, Lou & Sandy Whitehead purchased their first home at 42 S. Huron which was built in 1927. After looking at new homes in Grove City and as far north as housing developments near Rt. 161, they decided upon a home in Westgate. They liked the affordability and charm of the older homes and the easy commute to downtown. An added bonus was that Sandy's parents had recently purchased a home in Westgate. The Whiteheads raised their children Debbie and Scott here until 1982 when they moved to another Westgate house at 2937 Fremont St.

For the book, the three friends got together for coffee to discuss old memories. After several hours of "remembering," we decided not all could be documented for the WNA book but here are just a few:

Betsy's youngest daughter Valerie, Linda's daughter Cheri, and Sandy's daughter Debbie were the three musketeers. The girls spent many hours together playing between the three houses. During warm weather, Betsy's three-car garage was a favorite hang out.

Big Scott (Virden) and Little Scott (Whitehead) enjoyed the slope of the driveways to speed down into the street on their Big Wheels. Although the street is short and not a thru street, an elderly neighbor was quite concerned the boys might be hit by a car. The boys learned to make sharp right or left turns onto the sidewalk and avoid going into the street.

All of our children loved Westgate Park. The children fished, ice-skated and had fun on the swing sets. At the recreation center they enjoyed participating in classes such as ceramics, cooking and sewing as well as various indoor sports. An outdoor sport

The toy poodle, Taffy, belonged to Betsy. The dogs on the lower step were 2 of the 5 dogs adopted from Mr. Smith: Cleo (the Yorkie on the left) and Powder Puff (the Chihuahua on the right).

Scott Whitehead enjoyed was playing soccer while his friend Scott Virden watched or rode his bike. Easter Egg Hunts were fun events each year.

Betsy was very active in the Westgate Elementary Parent Teacher Association. Soon she encouraged Linda and Sandy to become active members. The three would spend many hours planning and working at school events.

Some of Betsy's fondest memories involved Robert Smith. Mr. Smith was a patient of Dr. Valko and an eccentric individual who always dressed in very bright colored matching outfits. This included his coats, hats, socks, shoes, sunglasses and, as Betsy learned after he died, his underwear. Mr. Smith loved his little dogs and owned both Yorkshire terriers and Chihuahuas. Many days he walked up and down W. Broad Street with as many as six of his dogs at a time and was always willing to stop and chat. Often he would board a bus with two of his dogs in a shopping bag and go downtown to Lazarus. What an attention getter, Mr. Smith dressed in one of his colored outfits with two unleashed little dogs following him! The women at the perfume counters loved the dogs and the dogs came home smelling wonderful and Mr. Smith with samples.

When Mr. Smith's health began to fail, he asked the Valkos if they would take in his little family of five dogs. Linda and Sandy have fun memories of Betsy walking the three Yorkies, two Chihuahuas and Taffy, her toy Poodle, on their twice-daily walks down S. Huron. What a sight they were!

Cowboy Hot Pot

Originally printed in the 2012 Westgate Home & Garden Tour booklet

Submitted by Robin Traxler

1. Chop, then fry the onion, pepper, and sweet potato or carrot until softened.
2. Add the green beans, baked beans, corn, tomato paste, and salt. Bring to a boil and simmer for 5 minutes.
3. Transfer the vegetables to a shallow pan and place the sliced cheese on top.
4. Cover the vegetable and cheese mixture with the sliced potatoes, brush with butter, season, and bake at 375 for 30-40 minutes until the potatoes are cooked and golden brown on top.

- 1 Onion
- 1 Red Bell Pepper
- 1 Sweet Potato or 2 Carrots
- 3 Tablespoons Oil
- 4 Ounces Smoked Cheese
- 4 Ounces Green Beans
- 1 Can Baked Beans
- 1 Can Corn
- 1 Tablespoon Tomato Paste
- 1 Teaspoon Salt
- 1 Pound Potatoes, thinly sliced
- 2 tablespoons Butter
- Salt & Pepper to taste

A Kid's Eye View of Westgate

Submitted by Judy (Rausch) Warner

In the 50s and 60s we had a great childhood in Westgate. What freedom we had. We walked or rode our bikes everywhere, anytime of the day. We delivered papers in the morning before daylight and after school. We had slumber parties and our parents didn't fear for us walking around the neighborhood after dark. In winter, we would go to Westgate Park and ice skate on the pond. The fire department would come over periodically and spray water on the skate rutted top so we could have a smooth surface. We warmed up by the fireplace in the shelter house near the pond. Once in a while we would even go ice-skating before school or go out for breakfast at a nearby restaurant. After school we played baseball, basketball, roller skated, rode bikes, visited with friends, and danced while watching Dick Clark's Dance Party on TV.

Milk Wagons & Air Raid Wardens

As told to Sandy Whitehead by Bob and Dee Smith

Bob Smith remembers when the milk delivery was by horse drawn wagons. He and friends were known to set off firecrackers to scare the horses. During WWII Bob was a Boy Scout. Scouts were messengers responsible for delivering notes to the Air Raid wardens during black outs. Each scout was assigned a white painted manhole cover along West Broad Street and once he received a message he ran it to the next white manhole. Bob also played soccer on the open field now Westgate school playground.

Dee Smith remembers when the milkmen put the bottles of milk in insulated enclosures built into the house. There was a door on the outside of the house which passed through to the kitchen.

Ice skating in Westgate Park, 1959

Sweet Memories of Cherry Cokes, Tennis & the Library

Submitted by Susie Loik Parsons

My parents purchased our home on South Huron Ave in 1960 for $16,000.

What I most remember about the home was the basement. It was cold and dark, with block walls with peeling paint. In the middle of the main room was an enormous furnace with low pipes you could bump your head on. My brother and I would roller skate around and around the furnace. I also remember being grossed out by the humongous black "water bugs." I just knew they could run fast and leap onto me!

I loved our big front porch and the big maple trees. I would play on the porch rain or shine in the summer, or sit and read books for hours.

The Hilltop Library at that time was at the corner of W. Broad Street and Binns Blvd. I would walk down the alley and spend hours there browsing through books, and reading on the green leather couches in front of the big front window. I felt safe going alone and Mom didn't worry about me. (My second job in high school was at this same library. I was paid $1.25 per hour!) Actually, I walked almost everywhere — to elementary, middle and then high school, the Post Office, stores, the bank, and to Great Western Shopping Center for ice cream at Islay's, go bowling, play miniature golf, or to see the Seven Wonders of the World display.

I have some great memories of neighborhood businesses:

Paul's Pharmacy was located on S. Westgate Avenue by the alley just south of W. Broad Street. Once my brother went with a friend who took a forged note "from his mom" requesting cigarettes for her. Paul called the mom and was told "No I didn't send my son for cigarettes."

Snyder's Furniture Store was a rather elegant shop located west of Westgate Avenue on Broad St. Mom had living room drapes made there in the 60's and they are still in fine shape! Next door was Haldeman Cleaners, where I took my dad's dress slacks.

And what kid could forget Etta at Haney's Drugs on W. Broad St.? Boy, we thought she was mean! Watched you like a hawk, even if you were a good kid. In summer it was a destination for my favorite treats: Cherry Cokes and hot fudge sundaes. I remember sitting at the counter on the swivel stools in the air conditioning. (We didn't have AC at home so it was quite a treat!)

Westgate Park was peaceful in the winter snow and vibrant with activity during the warmer months. In summer, the park offered softball leagues, concerts, and stone picnic tables to lie on and contemplate the trees and sky year-round. (The park was even home to a multi-day 3-wall handball tournament that drew players from neighboring states!) In winter we played ping-pong and pick-up basketball games in the rec center, and when the pond was safe for ice-skating, an attendant staffed the open shelter house and stoked the fire.

My very most favorite place in the park was the tennis courts! There was a wood hut inside the fence on the west side for the attendant. It also housed a pop machine and a phone. When the courts were crowded, especially in the evening, the attendant took reservations. If it was really crowded you were allotted only one hour of play. At that time there was no fee to play, but my mom, Nancy Hegwood Loik, remembers paying 10 cents a person for doubles and 15 cents a person for singles in 1940.

I began going there when I was about 13 years old with my friend, Janice Federer, to learn to play tennis. After a few frustrating weeks, Janice left me, but I was determined to learn how to play! I practiced daily, hitting against the walls of the handball courts. Over time I got to know the attendant, Bob Nash and other players. Bob taught me so much about the game and inspired a life-long love of tennis. For me it wasn't about winning it was about the feel of the movements and the positive flow of energy.

During my years at West High School, 1968–1970, there was no girl's tennis team. (There were very few organized girls sports in high schools then.) I was told by the administration that I couldn't play with the boys' tennis team because of the need for separate locker rooms. They didn't use a locker room! Bill White, the West High tennis coach, said I could practice with the team whenever I wanted, and I did.

Warming up in the Westgate Park open shelter after skating.

Every year the Recreation Department hosted the Gold Circle Tennis Tournament. At the height of its popularity the tournament drew more than 300 singles players. Matches were played at Westgate and other city parks. The fence at Westgate was lined with the brackets for each division. The attendants from each park would call match results to a central number; then the phone in the hut would ring and the brackets would be updated. Daily match scores were printed in *The Columbus Dispatch*. Trophies were awarded the winners.

Westgate on the Rise

Columbus Alive

From the February 16, 2012 edition

Reprinted with permission
Copyright 2012

Never heard of Westgate?

You'd have to see it to believe it.

Embedded in the gray, amorphous West Side, the residential enclave with cozy houses, tree-lined streets and close-knit community is luring young professionals looking to own their first homes.

"We were interested in Clintonville, but we couldn't really afford Clintonville," said Caleb Ely, who about a year ago moved to Westgate with his wife and two children. "Prices in Westgate were insanely reasonable."

Their story is common among Westgaters.

Turned away by prices elsewhere, the Elys heard about Westgate, stowed their wariness of the West Side and took a drive. Almost immediately, they fell in love with its quaint, inviting look and feel.

The area is bounded by South Hague Avenue on the east, Demorest Road on the west, West Broad Street on the north and Sullivant Avenue on the south.

"When we first moved in, we had neighbors bring over a welcome basket," Ely said. "We've met multiple friends just by walking on the street."

A welcome basket on the West Side? You'd have to receive it to believe it.

"A lot of us who have lived here for a while, if we have visitors who know Columbus, they are very surprised we're here," said Mari Ann Futty, a 14-year resident who serves as president of the Westgate Neighbors Association.

Many residents hope that the family-friendly neighborhood also becomes a great place to get a good cup of coffee, a delicious sit-down meal and a beer. They hope that an influx of creative professionals inspires commercial development along the West Broad and Sullivant corridors.

For now, Westgaters frequent a random collection of hidden restaurants, food carts and a great Mexican bakery attached to a drive-through beverage store.

Link to the complete story: http://www.columbusalive.com/content/stories/2012/02/16/city-westgate-on-the-rise.html

The photo on the left was a reenactment; the photo on the right was the real thing!

Civil War Encampment Reenactments

Submitted by Dick Hoffman

For five years during the 1980s history came alive when reenactments of a Civil War encampment were set up on the ball fields of St. Mary Magdalene School.

Both Confederate and Union reenactment units and individual interpreters put up rows of tents for sleeping, for supplies and for caring for the sick. It was a living history lesson of life during Camp Chase days. Infantry, artillery and medical units as well as camp followers and sympathizers gathered to give "first person accounts." Musicians played Civil War era music, there were medical demonstrations of the period, and children had fun learning marching drills using wooden rifles. Women demonstrated how to spin with spinning wheels and showed cooking skills over open fires in large kettles. Beans, no doubt, were cooked in many of the pots. During the last year of the encampment reenactments, an actual wedding took place on the traffic island in front of St. Mary Magdalene Church.

Grandfather Sold Goods to Camp Chase Soldiers

Submitted by Joanne Horn Hylton

By the time of the Civil War, James A. Fippin and his wife Mary Shank Fippin owned and lived on a 50-acre farm. The eastern boundary of the farm was at what is now Wilson Road.

Grandson Frank A. Sperry II wrote about the connection of the Fippin family to the area now known as the Westgate neighborhood:

Grandfather and grandmother Fippin lived all their lives on a 50 acre farm situated about a mile north of the National Pike on a road about a mile west of Hague Avenue, in Columbus, Ohio. The old red brick Quaker Church stands at the northwest corner of this road and the National Pike. They settled in a notable settlement of Quakers on the edge of Camp Chase. Camp Chase was one of the northern camps for the confinement of Confederate prisoners during the Civil War. A lot of grandfather's livelihood came from the sale of firewood and provisions to the camp. There is a story of the load of apples that were lost to him when one of the soldiers pulled out the end gate of his wagon scattering the apples to a free for all scramble.

Granddaughter Mary Catherine Sperry Hakola wrote of her mother, Mary Ann Fippin Sperry, daughter of James and Mary:

She often told of going with her father to sell buttermilk to the soldiers at nearby Camp Chase. One incident always amused us. When grandfather ran out of buttermilk, a soldier asked him if he had no water!! She also told us that her father hid his pigs under the cabin to keep the soldiers from stealing them.

Welcoming New Neighbors the Old Fashioned Way

Submitted by Betty Jaynes

Until 1998 Welcome Wagon hostesses visited new homeowners, telling them over a cup of coffee about local civic and cultural activities in the community while handing out gifts and coupons from local businesses.

In 2008 The Westgate Neighbors Association developed a new neighbor packet including information about the WNA, block watches, city services, and a list of businesses owned or operated by members of WNA.

Susie Parsons, WNA Membership Chairperson, watches the Dispatch for recent home sales in the neighborhood and has a group of volunteers personally deliver the packets.

New homeowners are encouraged to meet their neighbors at monthly Westgate Night Out (informal gatherings hosted in private homes and, occasionally restaurants), Mugs and Muffins (monthly Saturday morning events complete with coffee and pastries) or by attending a WNA meeting.

Westgate was actually featured in the August 28, 2011 Columbus Dispatch article titled Hello, Neighbor! The article highlighted communities (Westgate is one of the few in Columbus) that still strive to welcome newcomers with a personal greeting.

We like to think of Westgate not just as a development with 2,000 houses, but as a unique neighborhood. Call us old fashioned, but we believe this personal touch has helped to set us apart from many of the newer communities.

Adventures With Our Neighbors

Submitted by Debi Cunningham

When looking for our first home 33 years ago, we looked in many different locations, the suburbs & other city neighborhoods, and we found the most house for the money in Westgate.

What we found was a house with unique features such as "clock" or "watch steps" going to the second floor – they turn as they go to the second floor. The carpet installer told me the name - apparently they are a feature unique to older homes. Also, our hardwood floors are made from heartwood pine, which is no longer available.

But more than just a house, we found neighbors. One came to introduce herself and brought a pie. She happened to be a hair stylist and to this day I go to her salon.

For several years, when our children & our immediate neighbor's children were in elementary & middle school, we had our own special Fourth of July fireworks show. We lined the kids up in the back yard, behind the fence, and our fireworks "expert" (I won't say her name as I'm not sure the statute of limitations has expired) gave us a marvelous display. Most of them were shot from the alley or the concrete apron of another neighbor's garage, and we did have water handy just in case. We had a couple of near misses, which led to a collective decision to cease and desist in our illegal activities, but it was great fun while it lasted. We enjoyed some cool fireworks up close, and had a great time with our neighbors as well.

Westgate has been a wonderful place to live and raise a family. Our neighbors have been wonderful, helping us when we truly needed it. When our children were fairly young, we still had the old double-hung wooden windows, and no air conditioning. The frames of the windows would often get stuck. One summer, on an especially hot day, my husband was pounding on the window in our dining room in an attempt to get it to open further, hoping for more relief from the heat. He was unaware that our 2-year-old daughter had her fingers on the windowsill of the living room window, on the same wall. She was looking out of the window at the street. I don't remember if my husband's pounding was effective on the stuck window, but it caused the living room window to suddenly drop, clipping our daughter's finger. She wailed immediately, bringing our next door neighbor rushing over (thanks, Betty!). She said she could tell by the cry that our daughter was truly hurt. She stayed with our other two children and waited for my parents so we could run to the ER. It was comforting to know that we had neighbors who were so willing to help – even before we asked.

My most recent time of getting help from neighbors was when my main water line broke a few winters ago. Since it was below freezing, the Water Department had to shut off the water to keep the street from icing. Thanks again to my next door neighbors who filled buckets for me until I found an approved plumber & got the line fixed. Ah, the joys of owning an older home!

Westgate truly is a NEIGHBORhood.

Looking for Charlie the Catfish

Submitted by Linda Feigenbaum

Twelve years ago I was looking for a good elementary school for my then 4- year old grandson. We moved to the Westgate area to be close to Westgate Elementary School.

My grandson, Devon, remembers Miss Rosten, his first grade teacher, as being loving and caring. He credits Mr. Rinto, his 5th grade teacher, as having prepared him for middle school.

He also remembers spending hours at the park searching for Charlie the huge catfish. It might have only been an urban myth, but it sure was fun trying to find him.

The 1950 Snow Bowl

Submitted by Tom Christ

I was born and raised in Westgate. I attended St. Mary Magdalene and Aquinas High School.

We lived in the 400 block of Westgate Ave. directly across from what is now the Rec Center and have many fond memories of the park.

At one time the pond had casting rings we would use as targets to practice our casting.

In the winter we would ice skate on the pond and many families would bring their discarded Christmas trees to the shelter house so they could be burned in the fireplace. It was the perfect place to warm up while taking a break from skating.

I remember two large sledding hills on the south side of the park – winter was always fun.

Some might remember November 25, 1950 as the "1950 Snow Bowl." It was the worst blizzard in 37 years yet over 50,000 crazy fans braved the weather to watch Michigan beat Ohio State.

But that day I watched from my bedroom window as a group of teenagers rolled giant snowballs onto Westgate Ave. – blocking the street. The police were called, but by then the group had scattered. The police spent nearly an hour using their cruisers to break up the snowballs.

Did I mention that winter was always fun in Westgate?

Aunt Tammi's Park

Submitted by Tammi Gourley

My parents were high school sweethearts at West High School. As they started their family they bought their home on Roys – where I was raised, along with my brother and sister.

Growing up in Westgate in the 70's was wonderful. Some of my dear friends today are those I met while attending Westgate Elementary.

At West High my sister and I were varsity tennis players and my brother was a standout baseball player. But it is the Football Friday nights that were so memorable.

I was Homecoming Queen and loved riding a top a Corvette in the West High Homecoming Parade. That tradition carries on today as the band, the homecoming court, and floats travel through the streets of Westgate tossing candy to the children.

My parents' home is behind the football stadium, so when I hear

The scoreboard at West High School.

the marching band I get chills, as those great memories come flooding back.

After graduating from high school I left to attend Otterbein College. After college I bought a condo in Hilliard, but 8 years ago I was drawn back to Westgate.

My nieces call Westgate Park – "Aunt Tammi's Park" – and insist I take them there whenever they are in town. It is such a treasure to create some of the same memories with my nieces and nephew that my sister, brother and I had growing up.

I Believe That's My Dog You've Got There

Submitted by Mark, Kathy, and Nick Ingram, since July, 1995

We have lived in Westgate since our son was one year old. We moved from the east side of Columbus to the west side because our very good friend told us what a great area it was. Her parents told us that home values have increased for the past sixty years. That sounded good to us and we loved the neighborhood as we drove through it looking for houses. The biggest draw for us to move to Westgate was the multitude of different style houses. We love looking at all the different architectural designs.

The house we found is all red brick with a front porch and unattached garage. It was built in 1948. The house has lots of old-fashioned touches. We have a telephone nook built into the dining room's wall. In addition to the many arched doorways, we have French glass doors from the dining room into what we call the computer room. Our front door is a beautiful walnut wood. Our mailbox is built into the house so you can place and receive mail from inside.

My most special memory from living in Westgate occurred when our son, Nick, was in Cub Scouts and I took them to the Fire Station. They had so much fun playing on the fire trucks and blowing the horns. We also love going to Westgate Park, not only for the Bean Dinner, but for the walking trail and playground equipment. The yard sales on the Hilltop Bean Dinner Saturday are exceptional as a large percentage of homes participate and there are always great finds.

There is a real sense of community in Westgate where we walk up and down the streets with our dogs. Everyone is friendly and we often stop and catch up on neighborhood news. Our last dog was so friendly that one time when he got away from us and we went looking for him, we found him on a leash walking with another woman. She said he came right up, happy as can be, and allowed her to put him on the leash.

Our son attended middle school at St. Mary Magdalene and then onto high school at Bishop Ready. We have many memories of the two schools with all the after-school activities and friends we have found. Even though our son is now in college, we still buy from Market Day to support St. Mary Magdalene.

A Near Miss

As told to Sandy Whitehead by Carol Nation

Carol's daughter Kari delivered papers from the time she was twelve years old until the age of eighteen. Each morning they got up at 5:30 a.m. for Kari to begin her route. Most mornings nothing extraordinary happened. However, there was the morning soon after Kari began driving her route. She forgot to put the car in park. The car began moving down Fremont St. across Binns Blvd. and thankfully stopped before hitting a parked truck.

the Westgate Derby Day Dash

In 2010, The Westgate Neighbors Association sponsored an event that was a "twist" on the traditional house and garden tour. The Derby Day Dash, held on May 1st (Kentucky Derby Day), was a progressive cocktail party held at six houses. Each house spotlighted a past Kentucky Derby winner and featured themed foods and drinks.

Secretariat House
152 South Westgate Avenue
1973 Triple Crown Winner

Hosts: Betty & Jerry Jaynes

Menu: Sweet Treats

Beverages: JW Dundees Honey Brown & CBC Apricot Ale from Hill Distributing; Coffee courtesy of Milo's Deli; Assorted Liqueurs from Europia

Barbaro House
80 South Algonquin Avenue
2006 Kentucky Derby Winner

Hosts: Walter Tucker & Ruben Nieto

Corporate Sponsor: Hill Distributing

Menu: Mexican Fiesta courtesy of Famosa and Casa Sazon

Beverages: Negra Modelo & Pacifico from Hill Distributing

Seattle Slew House
170 South Huron Avenue
1977 Triple Crown Winner

Host: Sarah Fairchild

Menu: Asian Fare courtesy of Luc's Asian Market

Beverages: Shiner Bock & Red Stripe Light from Hill Distributing; Plum Wine from Europia; Cherry Lambic Vodka Punch made with sorbet courtesy of Jeni's Ice Creams

Whiskery House
34 South Roys Avenue
1927 Kentucky Derby Winner

Host: LeNan Empey

Menu: Kentucky Derby Traditions courtesy of Casserole Girl Catering

Beverages: O'Fallon's Wheach & Smirnoff Ice; Blueberry Lemonade from Hill Distributing; Bourbon Cocktails

Smarty Jones House
104 South Roys Avenue
2004 Kentucky Derby Winner

Host: Alan Jazak

Corporate Sponsor: U.S. Bank, Westland Office

Menu: Italian Picnic courtesy of Spinelli's Deli

Beverages: Stella Artois & Warsteiner Dunkle from Hill Distributing; Mint Juleps courtesy of Spinelli's Deli

Sir Barton House
2911 Crescent Drive
1919 The very FIRST Triple Crown Winner

Host: Kathleen Conlon

Menu: Wine & Cheese Selections

Beverages: Guinness Beer & Bass Ale from Hill Distributing; White & Red Wines from Europia

The 2011 Westgate Home and Garden Tour

The WNA began sponsoring neighborhood home and garden tours in 2011. The unique aspect of the Westgate Tour is that while the homes and gardens may be smaller in size and expense compared to other "tour-worthy" neighborhoods in Columbus, our properties abound with affordable, doable design ideas, and efficient, creative uses for the modest indoor and outdoor spaces found here.

2959 Crescent Dr.
Dutch Colonial
built 1927 · 1,911 sq. ft.

240 S. Westmoor Ave.
Tudor Revival
built 1936 · 1,888 sq. ft.

106 Binns Blvd.
Colonial Revival
built 1940 · 1,700 sq. ft.

196 S. Algonquin Ave.
Colonial Revival
built 1948 • 1,380 sq. ft.

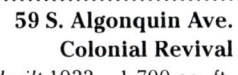

59 S. Algonquin Ave.
Colonial Revival
built 1933 • 1,700 sq. ft.

92 S. Powhatan Ave.
Tudor Revival
built 1930 • 1,500 sq. ft.

255 S. Westmoor Ave.
Tudor Revival
built 1940 • 1,816 sq. ft.

3051 Palmetto St.
Tudor Revival/English Cottage Variant
built 1950 • 1,500 sq. ft.

105 Binns Blvd.
Dutch Colonial
built 1928 • 1,840 sq. ft.

Good Karma in Westgate

Submitted by Matt & Alisa Hazelbaker

We looked at houses throughout Columbus, trying to find something that fit our dream ... the dream of a move-in-ready older home! After tirelessly searching and not finding anything that fit, a friend from work suggested the Westgate neighborhood. After work that night, Alisa & I took a drive through the neighborhood and were intrigued. We called our real estate agent and promptly began looking at homes in the area. When we found our home, we knew it was the perfect one for us – a 1920's craftsman style home with new floors, new windows, new kitchen, and lots of space. The rest as they say, is history.

When we compared ours to the homes of our friends outside of Westgate, we found our home to be dynamically different. From the craftsman built-in cabinets beside our fireplace to the original wood trim and banister to the gorgeous archways and architecture, our house stands alone.

But our love of Westgate goes beyond our physical house. When we moved in, we were immediately greeted and welcomed to the neighborhood. We were given a welcome basket and invited to a Christmas gathering, giving us a chance to meet more of our neighbors. At the same time, we signed up for a neighborhood email distribution list to keep us informed of various "goings on." In a world so disconnected by modern life, this warm welcome spoke volumes and reassured us of our choice to settle in the Westgate neighborhood. The deep sense of pride and community felt by our neighbors is something we hope to carry on throughout our years in this neighborhood.

Another important memory is our first real Halloween in the house. When we moved into the home in 2007, it was late October, and we had so much to do around the house (painting, etc.) that we had to miss the first Halloween here. However, the following year, we were shocked and excited to see the incredible number of kids and families that visit our neighborhood to "trick or treat." Vampires and princesses and bears (oh my) stopped by our door to get candy throughout the evening. Even Mayor Coleman stopped by Westgate. We passed out all of our candy within 45 minutes! We quickly discovered that the real "trick" to Halloween in Westgate is making sure you have enough treats to last the night!

Memories From My Schooldays

Submitted by Elizabeth Hylton

I lived in Westgate from the age of 4 until the age of 21 so I have many pleasant memories of Westgate.

I attended Westgate Elementary School back in the 1960s. Several annual school events stand out in my memories. One event was the Halloween Parade. The entire student body including some of the faculty would dress up in Halloween costumes. All of the grades were assigned by groups and would be allowed to parade throughout the entire school and around the school grounds modeling their costumes. As I recall, there was a best costume award. One memorable costume was a large pumpkin suit made by a mother for a classmate. When the parade ended we went back to our classrooms for a Halloween Party.

Another event was Fun Night. Fun Night occurred on a Friday night in the fall and was sponsored by the PTA. There were a variety of activities such as the ring toss, guessing games, and the fish pond which was particularly popular. One year, my brother won a goldfish at the fish pond which, of course, he named Goldie.

Another enjoyable game was the cake walk. It was a variation of musical chairs and the last person sitting in the chair would win a cake. One year, our next-door neighbors each won a cake and shared their winnings with us.

Westgate: Land of Milk and Honey

Submitted by Steve Stone

As a child growing up in the 1950's on the Hilltop's Steele Avenue, I attended West Broad Street Elementary School from kindergarten through the sixth grade. My principal, Forrest Rader, lived on North Warren in the same neighborhood. While I didn't think of myself as poor, I knew we didn't have a lot of money and I thought it odd that a school principal would live in my neighborhood. I knew, though, where people with good jobs and a lot of money would live and that was Westgate!

The Mayor, M.E. "Jack" Sensenbrenner, lived there. Mack Pemberton, our state representative, Mr. McCallister, principal of Westmoor Junior High and Dave Randall, West High's principal also lived in Westgate. Mr. Wills, a teacher at Westmoor, lived in a really nice, well-kept house on South Southampton. Yes, people of importance, with good jobs and lots of money surely must live in Westgate.

How did I know? Because my Dad said so! He asked the mayor once to pave the alley that ran the length of our yard beside our house with chip and seal topping. As I remember, he claimed the mayor told him that if he did that, our alley would be better than the alleys in Westgate. That set my Dad to ranting about "Westgate people thinking they were better" than those of us living to the east on the Hilltop.

One day, my boyhood friend who lived next door told me he was moving away. "We're moving to Westgate," his mother said with a smile of achievement and great satisfaction. Then she added insult to injury and said, "We'll be glad to get out of this neighborhood."

From my 5th grade classroom, I could look out of the windows and see Georgiton's Restaurant on the corner of Broad and Hague. Just west of that intersection was the Roush Brother's Hardware Store full of all manner of fancy tools and sporting goods like bicycles, skates and sleds. Traveling west on Broad Street, it only got better from there as you approached the Westgate neighborhood. I remember two perfectly groomed businessmen, Joe Worthen, a tailor and high-end men's clothing store owner, along with Dick Haldeman, the dry cleaner who always was in a suit and tie. Always! There was Louie Leaman, our dentist and his office assistant wife with the barky little dog. Louis grew up in Buchtel, a southeast Ohio hard scrabble coal mine town. Somehow, I knew he was glad not to be there; a poor boy who had reached the pinnacle of success as a dentist in Westgate.

At Christmas, my Dad would pile us in the family car and we'd drive around Westgate to look at the plethora of Christmas lights. It was an annual treat and the place to go for the best holiday decorations. When we decorated our house, the standard was always "it looks as good as the houses in Westgate!"

So, it only made sense that when my wife, Jan, who moved to Westgate in the 3rd grade, and I returned home from the Army in 1972, we would set our sights on a house in Westgate. We were,

I think, the youngest people on our street and over the years we watched old businesses close, people die or move away to Upper Arlington or other suburbs farther from the city and new folks move in.

The house across the street from us where Dr. and Mrs. John Thompson raised their family and lived in quiet dignity until old age took them away, has been sold to new people several times. But to us, it is still "Dr. Thompson's house!" And neighbors up the street have lived for years in homes we sometimes refer to as Pemberton's or the Judge Thatcher's house.

I wonder if a new generation of homeowners will stay around long enough to have their home assume their family's name or one day look at our house and say, "Oh that's the Stone house! Remember them?"

Growing Up on Brinker

Submitted by Keri (Muller) Wilson

I have so many fond memories growing up on Brinker in the 1980s. I would ride to Rax at the corner of Brinker and Broad (now an Enterprise Rental Car location.)

Whenever I had extra money I would ride my bike down to Mike's Carryout at the corner of Huron and Sullivant to buy candy. While not the penny candy my parents grew up with, I still could buy an entire bag of candy with my dollar.

I took ceramic classes at Westgate Rec Center and to this day my mother still has these works of art.

I attended St. Mary Magdalene and then Bishop Ready High School. Westgate was a wonderful neighborhood to grow up and a great place to bring my kids to visit their grandparents and the park.

The 2012 Westgate Home and Garden Tour

You just never know what's around the corner when you come to visit Westgate. Guests at the 2012 tour stepped into the past when they walked into an unassuming looking Cape Cod on Algonquin Avenue. The interior – from fixtures to floors to furnishings – was all done in 1940s style, big band music played on the stereo, and even the tour volunteers got into the act by dressing in period costumes.

2959 Palmetto St.
Tudor Revival
built 1939 · 1,593 sq. ft.

3027 Crescent Dr.
Dutch Colonial Revival
built 1927 · 1,696 sq. ft.

2930 Crescent Dr.
Dutch Colonial Revival
built 1926 · 1,588 sq. ft.

37 S. Sylvan Ave.
Colonial Revival with First Period Influences
built 1937 · 1,516 sq. ft.

207 Powhatan Ave.
Colonial Revival Cape Cod
built 1947 · 1,650 sq. ft.

3107 Ellis Pl.
American Foursquare
built 1928 · 1,472 sq. ft.

44 S. Sylvan Ave.
Character Ranch with Tudor Influences
built 1947 · 2,513 sq. ft.

65 S. Algonquin Ave.
Colonial Revival with Tudor Revival Influences
built 1928 · 1,380 sq. ft.

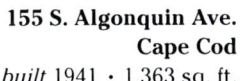

155 S. Algonquin Ave.
Cape Cod
built 1941 · 1,363 sq. ft.

The Westgate Toll Path Trail

Submitted by Tom Ongaro

During the hot summer of 1947 my childhood neighbor friend, Dick Price, and I both lived on Letchworth Avenue in Westgate.

Because of the new homes being built in this neighborhood, many of the lots were vacant fields loaded with tall grass and thistle weeds, which made it almost impossible for anyone to walk between Letchworth and Southampton Avenues. We were thirteen years old and we wanted to do something good for our neighborhood so we came up with the idea of blazing a walking path through the field. We decided to connect these two streets and then neighbors could use this to take a shortcut to the end of the bus line on Southampton Ave. instead of having to walk down to Olive and Southampton and back up to West Broad to catch the bus. People who did try to walk through the field would get burrs of weeds on their clothing, and were bitten by insects and blocked by huge spider webs.

Dick and I got our push mowers and sickles and started clearing a ziz-zag, winding path, cutting down weeds that towered over our heads. It took a whole week to blaze this trail. We cut a five-foot swath and removed the weeds. By 1:00 p.m., we would head for the Hilltop Swimming pool on our bikes and then continue the next day.

We would direct people getting off the buses to the path where we posted a sign that read, "Toll Path," 10c but many people gave us more than a dime.

Dick Price carried one lady's groceries on his bike and escorted her home. He refused to charge her for the extra service. Eventually we stopped charging, patrolled the path on our hikes, and escorted people for free.

Today Camp Chase Drive is connected by an alley to Southampton Ave. and now there is no longer a toll path. I guess we were the Lewis and Clark of Westgate.

"U.S. Army Convoy Camps in Westgate"

I was nine years old in 1943 when I saw a convoy of U.S. Army jeeps and trucks loaded with soldiers coming from the west on US Route 40, (West Broad St.), towing trailers with containers of water, fuel and small artillery cannons. They came under the New York Central railroad bridge then turned right off West Broad and camped in a vacant field on Camp Chase Drive, which is parallel to Broad Street in Westgate. Derrer Road, Letchworth and Demorest Avenues led into Camp Chase.

In the vacant field, the soldiers set up their pup tents and parked their equipment under the very large and tall Norway spruce trees. Those trees were so full of branches that I could play under them and not get wet from rain. The soldiers were heading east to New York and beyond as one soldier told me. I was so excited to see so much action going on but hardly heard any loud noises from them. They told me they were coming from the Western States, but that was it.

In July 1944 Tom and Mrs. Rose organized a paper drive to support local efforts duirng World War II..

I remember all this because I was playing in the area before they arrived. I ran a half block to my home on Letchworth and put on my Army hat, belt, water canteen and a toy pistol with holster. I saluted myself in the dining room mirror and went back to visit those soldiers. I was so excited. Before they asked me to go home and just as it was getting dark, a group of soldiers asked me why this street was named Camp Chase Drive. They questioned why there weren't any signs of barracks. I was nine years old; the only thing I could tell them was this area was part of a northern army camp, there was a prison close to a cemetery on Sullivant, and that it had something to do with the Civil War. The next day I walked over the campsite and the soldiers and trucks were gone. I was very sad, but I can say that I was dressed in Military form and gave my first talk about Camp Chase.

The Day the Attic Attacked Me

Submitted by Lisa (Prince) Harrison

Even though I did not officially "grow up" in Westgate, it has been a part of my life almost since birth. My grandparents owned a twin single on Westgate Ave. when I was born; they lived in one side and rented the other side out. My parents rented a house at 313 S. Sylvan Ave., where I lived until I was 3, and then my grandparents owned the house at 3425 Wicklow Rd., at the southeast corner of Derrer Rd.

The Wicklow house was what I believe is referred to as a "story and a half," meaning there was an attic upstairs that you could almost, but not quite, walk upright in. I remember it had a row of hardwood storage cabinets that were built into the wall, and ran the length of the front of the house. One time I locked myself in the cabinets and was petrified. It seemed like I was in there forever before my grandmother found me, and that is probably where my claustrophobia could be traced to. I will NEVER forget that attic!...up until then it like having a huge playhouse of my own because it wasn't quite big enough for "the grownups" to hang out in but it was perfect for a 4-year-old and all the toys that came with one.

We were two houses away from the park and it seemed like miles to get to the "kiddie playground" over by the rec center. My favorite playground toy was a yellow elephant slide with red spots on it. It was small but seemed like the perfect size back then, as it wasn't reallllly high like the one over at the "big kids'" park.

After I was older and we had moved over off of Eakin Rd., I used to go to school from my babysitter's house and that's how I ended up at Westgate Elementary in 5th grade. I thought my teacher Mrs. Cassady was just the prettiest teacher in the world and she was so cool. She was young, and had long blonde hair. She was the first teacher I ever really felt like I could relate to....

By 6th grade, my best friend and I used to go to the dances at the rec center on Friday nights. I remember learning my first "cool" dance there to the song "Rock With You" by Michael Jackson. We thought we were very big and grown up and would walk home to her house on Roys Ave. at (gasp!) 10 o'clock when the dance would let out.

After I grew up and had babies of my own I used to turn them loose in the kiddie playground while I would sit on the bench and remember spending my pre-kindergarten afternoons there. They used to love it as much as I did, and nobody ever wanted to go home. We would pack a bag with snacks and drinks and stay all afternoon. Those were great times that I look back fondly on now that they are all grown up.

Happy & Free, That Was Me!

Submitted by Ann Daniels

I grew up just outside the boundaries of Westgate and have many fond memories of the area.

In elementary school I would visit Jan Deitrick and we would go to Haney's and the old Big Bear to snoop around. I believe we even put handkerchiefs on our heads and went to St. Mary Magdalene one day.

In the summers during high school years, I would spend the day over in the West High area — going to band practice, taking driver's education and working a few hours at the YMCA in the little snack area close to the ball fields.

I enjoyed walking through all parts of Westgate Park — when my mom wanted to get rid of my brother and I, she would give us strips of bacon and send us over to go fishing at the pond for a few hours.

I remember many Bean Dinners — looking forward to what friends you would go with and who you would see. One memorable time I managed to barf up my beans on a nauseating capsule ride.

Remembering those days, I am struck by how much I was out and about — usually walking to school or walking to a friend's house. I felt comfortable and happy to be free to go wherever I wanted.

Hussey Family Came to Westgate in 1800s

Submitted by Sandy Whitehead

After 1870 when the U.S. Government abandoned the Camp Chase Civil War Camp land, Quakers breaking away from the large Quaker settlement in Jefferson County purchased land for $187.50 per acre.

John Hussey purchased land in the same area after 1872. His home stood in the 3100 block of West Broad Street across from the present day Chase bank. Many years later, decedents of John, Gray & Alice Hussey, lived only a few blocks away at 3006 Crescent Dr.

Soup Roast

Alice Hussey RECIPE

1 (3 lb) round steak (2 in. thick)

1 pkg. dry onion soup mix

1 can cream of mushroom or cream of chicken soup

Cover bottom of roasting pan with foil, leaving a generous overlap.

Sprinkle ½ the package dry soup and ½ can of condensed soup over foil.

Lay meat on top of the mixture and sprinkle remaining dry and condensed soup on top of the meat.

Fold the foil together to seal airtight.

Bake 3 hours at 300°.

Peanut Butter Pie

Alice Hussey Recipe

1 Graham Cracker Crust

½ cup of Peanut Butter *(crunchy is best)*

3 ounces of cream cheese

1 cup of Powdered Sugar

1 teaspoon of Vanilla

8 or 9 ounces of Cool Whip

Cream together the cheese and sugar.

Add vanilla and mix well. Put into crust.

Chill at least 2 hours.

Moving To Westgate

Submitted by Sally and Bob Yocom

Sally and I came to Columbus after my discharge from the Army in 1955. I had a job waiting for me from J.C. Penney at 106 N. High St. I had seen a college buddy while I was in the Army, and he told me about a new apartment building complex at Westgate Manor. We liked the area, and the park, and have bought two houses in the Westgate area since we moved from the apartment in 1959.

Sally has not only written stories, but currently is interested in writing poetry, and belongs to an International group which critiques each others' works. This group has awarded her numerous First Place commendations for her work.

Pumpkin Cheesecake Bars

Submitted by Ric Brandel

CRUST

1 c. flour	½ c. brown sugar
5 T. butter (cold)	½ c. chopped pecans

Combine flour and brown sugar; cut in butter until crumbly. Stir in chopped nuts. Reserve ¾ c. of crumbs for topping; press the remaining crumb mixture into an 8-inch baking pan. Bake at 350 degrees for 15 minutes.

FILLING

8 ounces softened cream cheese

½ c. canned pumpkin	¾ c. sugar
1-½ tsp. cinnamon	2 beaten eggs
1 tsp. vanilla	1 tsp. allspice

Combine filling ingredients and pour over crust. Sprinkle the reserved crumbs overtop; bake at 350 degrees for 35-40 minutes.

TEXAS SHEET CAKE

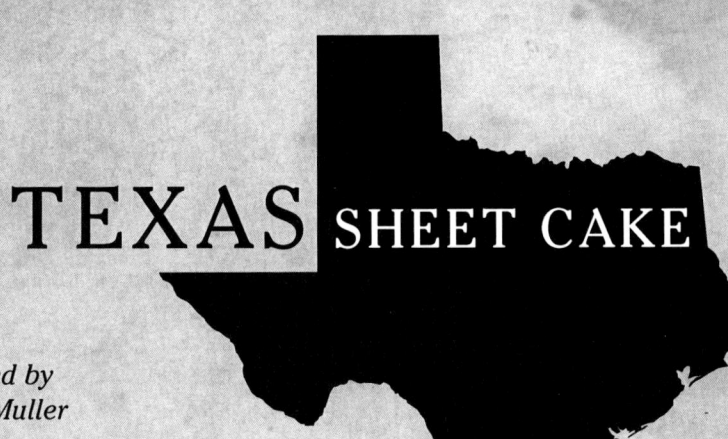

Submitted by
Sharon Muller

2 sticks margarine	2 cups flour
1 cup water	2 cups sugar
4 tbsp. cocoa	½ tsp. salt
2 eggs	½ cup sour cream
1 tsp. baking soda	

1. Bring margarine, water and cocoa to a boil
2. Remove from heat and add flour, sugar and salt
3. Beat in eggs, sour cream and baking soda
4. Pour into greased cookie sheet or jelly roll pan.

Bake at 375 for 17 minutes.

The Frosting:

1 stick margarine	3 tbsp. cocoa
6 tbsp. milk	1 lb. (3 ¾ c) powdered sugar
Chopped walnuts	

1. Bring margarine, cocoa and milk to a boil
2. Add powdered sugar

Pour frosting over cake and top with chopped walnuts.

Dahlen Family in Westgate Since 1929

Submitted by Deborah Dahlen Buzard, Scott Buzard, Jamie Buzard, Hannah Buzard

Ernest and Margaret Dahlen, Sr., my father's parents came to Westgate in 1929. My father Ernest (Ernie) L. Dahlen, Jr. grew up on S. Westmoor.

My mother's parents, Bess and Walter Kietzman moved here in 1947. My mother, Shirley M. Kietzman, attended West High School for her senior year.

My parents met after high school, dad being 5 years older. My mother and dad brought me to my Grandparents' house on Crescent Drive when I was born because their apartment was too hot in July in Grandview. My brothers and I spent many weekends at Mommer and Papa's house and have lots of fond memories.

Scott's mother and aunt, Shalmir Springer Buzard and Shirley Springer Duval, grew up on S. Brinker and graduated from West High School. They knew my parents and several of my parents' friends.

Scott spent a great deal of his childhood riding his bike to Westgate Park and cruising the alleys when visiting his grandparents. We discovered it truly is a small world.

I grew up in a suburb of Columbus, but have lived on Crescent Drive since 1982 after moving back to Columbus from Lexington, Kentucky where I attended UK.

My husband, Scott and I, too, brought our children, Jamie and Hannah home from the hospital to Crescent Drive. This home has been in our family for 65 years.

Raising our children on Crescent Drive has been an adventure. Many other young families had children about the same time. At one time there were over 15 children being raised on our street.

As parents we were always outside in the warm weather watching our children and having "adult" conversation. We went to Chuck E Cheese, the Zoo, and Hilltop pool together. Our kids had friends right outside their door and could walk down the street to have a great day.

At one point during the raising of all of our "kids" a neighbor's sister called Crescent Drive "Mayberry." We enjoyed the Crescent Drive Block party (1993–2007) and would close down our block the Saturday before school started for an all-day event ending with flashlight tag at night for the kids (and some adults).

In 1993 during the Holidays we began having a Progressive Dinner at 3 homes. We still have this event today on a smaller scale.

Raising our family in Westgate and on Crescent Drive has provided our children, now 21 and 18 years old, the opportunity to grow up in a safe community that is diversified and has given them the foundation to grow and mature into young adults. Raising them in this home has given them a sense of family history. They, too, feel the eternal spirit of Mommer, my grandmother, who can be felt during the tough times giving us the strength to move forward.

Brussels Sprouts in Garlic & Butter

Our family has shared Christmas dinner for the past 9 years around the corner with the Futtys.

I take this dish every year. Simple yet delicious and our kids even like it!

Cut Brussels sprouts in half and sauté with butter and fresh chopped garlic. Allow to brown slightly.

Corn Pudding

My grandmother, Bess Kietzman, made this for many family dinners.

2 bags whole kernel corn
2 eggs
1 ¼ c milk
3 Tbsp. flour
1 stick butter, melted

Cook corn. Mix eggs, butter, milk and flour and combine with corn.
Pour into buttered 13 x 9 dish and bake at 350.
This will come out as a pudding and is very good.

You can vary ingredient amounts to suit your needs.

The Blizzard of '77

As told to Sandy Whitehead by Tom Wire

Tom attended Westgate Elementary in the 1970s and recalls the blizzard of 1977. The school was closed for days giving him and his buddies an opportunity to build snow tunnels. After shoveling the snow into drifts of around five feet, they made a tunnel system through the whole backyard. After several days with below zero temperatures, his mom forbade Tom to play outdoors.

Westgate Elementary was closed during the winter of 1977 due to the natural gas shortage and Tom remembers attending classes at Hoge Presbyterian for several weeks before moving back to the Westgate Elementary classrooms.

Westgate During the 1940s

As told to Sandy Whitehead by Doris Fahrenback

Doris' parents moved to 128 Westgate Ave. in 1936. Her husband and she moved in with them in 1940. Doris walked on Olive to the bus stop. She remembers that at Christmas the neighborhood was aglow with outdoor Christmas lights on most of the homes. Doris said the house on the southeast corner of Binns and Olive was especially beautiful. She and her husband moved to a double located on S. Huron in 1943.

Coming into Westgate from the west in the 1940s, the city reminded drivers to slow down.

Doris remembers skating after dark on Westgate pond and maintaining a Victory Garden plot where Westgate Elementary School playground is now located.

Neighbors Accepting of "Mr. Mom'

Submitted by Patrice Ross

My Westgate memory is quite typical, I expect, with a bit of an unexpected twist (just like the neighborhood itself!). We – myself, husband Stan and our two children, then a toddler and a baby, were looking for a home to purchase in 1992. While there were two adults in the household, we were at that point a one-income family and we found the houses in Westgate to be both charming and affordable. The home we found needed some tender loving care but it had a beautiful fireplace, a screened porch and both an attic and basement – just right for a our family (and affordable on a single paycheck!). So, we bought the house, repapered the walls, replaced the old furnace, and moved in. Then I went back to work, and Stan stayed home with the babies.

We were a role-shift family before it was very common. Stan took the kids to the park, read them stories before their naps, got supper started and went along on elementary-school field trips. Although this arrangement is more common now, when we were living this life, it was still rather unusual. However, it was readily accepted by our families and neighbors as well. And, I suppose this is really the essence of my Westgate story: on one hand, we lived a lifestyle that might have been typical for a generation or more before the 1990's. Our children grew up playing softball and baseball at Westgate Park and St. Mary Magdalene. They biked and roller-skated over to the library and to the Dairy Twist. They participated in Scouts here, took various classes at the rec. center and even found a lead musket ball while helping me plant a flowerbed at our house. (Yes, we do still have it and yes, it is definitely a piece of lead shot such as was in use during the Civil War!). Sometimes we walked to our church in the neighborhood. And yet, it wasn't really the 1950s in the 1990s. They had a stay-at-home dad until they were 9 and 10 years old. So, for me, that really typifies Westgate – a place to raise a family, just like the old days, except new twists on old themes are readily accepted, just as we were when we moved here.

My Memories Begin in the 1930s

As told to Sandy Whitehead by Bill Gardner

Bill's parents were the second owners of 152 Powhatan. Born in 1932, Bill attended West Broad Elementary and graduated from West High. For thirty years, his father worked as a movie projector man for the Palace Theater and during World War II, served as an Air Warden. During blackouts, Bill can remember his father going out the door, wearing his helmet with his whistle around his neck and carrying his gas mask.

Bill recalled a field of clover near his home plowed by a horse called Dolly. They never cleared the streets of ice or snow enabling the children to ice-skate on them each winter. He is unsure of the years, but recalled when Pepsi distributed free samples to the homes in Westgate. Kids also enjoyed eating chunks of ice obtained from trucks delivering ice for iceboxes.

The Bean Dinner was a big event. Each year Bill enjoyed watching the men set up rides in the area of the Westgate tennis courts. He recalled a severely handicapped man named Les who drove a specially made motorized car. From an attached wagon, Les sold candy and trinkets.

Bill recalled the businesses on West Broad. Luckup's Drug store at the corner of Westgate, Huntz Market at Powell, a dairy at Westmoor and located in what is now Haldeman Cleaners area was the Red & White Market. The intersection of Sylvan and Palmetto was zoned for commercial businesses. The only businessperson to take advantage of the commercial intersection was Max Snavely. He owned an auto repair shop located in his oversized garage on the N.W. corner. Max was a good mechanic and Bill took all his cars to him for any repairs.

He remembers several Westgate residents. Jimmie Hill, who lived at 63 Powhatan, was the first director of the West High Band to take them to the Rose Bowl Parade in January 1969. NASA astronaut, Donn Eisele, attended West High and occupied the command module pilot seat for the eleven-day flight of Apollo 7. Jim Cooper broadcasted on WBNS radio from his home on Binns Blvd.

Bill Gardner remembers the proud day when the West High School Band marched in the 1969 Rose Bowl Parade.

My Upper Arlington

Submitted by Denise Schwaigert

I have lived on the West Side most of my life. Growing up I always thought of Westgate as "my Upper Arlington." I thought that if I lived there, that would mean that you have made it in life. I have lived in Westgate now 23 years. I wouldn't live anywhere else. I tried to live in Hilliard and Plain City but was never happy. I never felt that I fit in. Westgate is my home and I am especially happy here.

The Flood of '59

Submitted by Linda Barnhart Lowry

I lived in the Westgate area from the time I was in kindergarten until I got married 41 years ago. My family lived at 353 S. Algonquin Ave. until selling the house to Parkview Methodist Church. We moved one street over to 328 Powhatan Ave. while I was attending and graduated from Franklin University in 1969. I lived with my folks until I got married in February of 1971. My mother (Helen Mitten Barnhart) passed away in 1977 and my father (Clarence Ray Barnhart) passed away in 1981. Their house on Powhatan was sold about a year after Dad passed away.

I graduated from Westgate Elementary School; Westmoor Junior High School (graduated in 1962) and West High School (graduated in 1965).

Memories of Westgate School

I started at Westgate in the middle of kindergarten. My teacher was Mrs. Oliver.

Once a year there was Fun Night at school. Lots of games to play, good food.

We went home for lunch. No formal cafeteria.

Mrs. Laird was my 3rd and 4th grade teacher. What an inspiration she was to me. One of my favorite teachers. Mr. Phillips was my 6th grade teacher. He used to let me clean the chalkboard all the time. He was a very caring teacher.

Flood of 1959 – rain came down so hard that water was leaking through new flat roof. Trashcans were placed everywhere. School let out early. Teachers walked students to crosswalk and helped us get across the flooded streets. We were told to go directly home. My mother met us with our boots and took us across Brinker and Algonquin to our house. Remember helping Mom move stuff up to safe places in basement. Dad called to make sure we got home ok and made sure we wore our boots in flooded basement to help Mom. Frightening for all of us.

Music classes were offered to students who were interested. That is where I learned to play my dad's small violin. Then went on to my dad's big violin and carried over to Westmoor Jr. High School.

West High Homecoming — 1960

Memories of West High School

The stadium was full every game. Parking was very hard to find. There was a very large Marching Band and a large group of Weskets.

Polio Vaccine – oral vaccine was given out at the school for all families. We would stand in line for our dose. Think we had to go a couple of times.

Lunch – ate at school. A carton of milk was like 5 or 10 cents out of the vending machines. There were no pop machines. After lunch could go to the auditorium to watch a movie for a small fee. Sometimes held a sock hop in the gym.

There were many groups you could belong to, most met before school.

Hilltop Relays – was a big thing that was held at the stadium. Other schools came to compete.

Graduation – we had 500 graduates in my class of 1965. Graduation was held in the stadium. There was also a Bacheloria Service on Sunday at the school before graduation.

Memories of the old Hilltop Library

I started to work there when I was 16 years old after school.
I worked there until one year out of high school. A lot of the girls in my neighborhood worked there as Pages. Pages worked after school 2 nights a week from 4 p.m. until 9 p.m. Then we worked either Friday night or all day on Saturday every other week.
We got paid 95 cents an hour starting out. Then got 5-cent raises periodically. We read the shelves (made sure books were where they were supposed to be in order); checked in books; helped librarians as needed; made sure tables were cleaned off and chairs put under them.

Memories of Parkview United Methodist Church

We lived across from the church at 353 S. Algonquin Ave. from the time I was in elementary school until I was halfway thru college. I attended Bible School there.

Church was named Westgate Methodist Church when we moved to our house. Top of church was added on while we lived at our house. Was very interesting to watch the work being done.

We could sit on our front porch and watch all wedding groups coming out.

I remember people coming out of church commenting on my beautiful flowers and morning glories I had planted. They especially loved my morning glories climbing up the strings I had placed at the side of the porch.

Parkview Methodist Church bought our house and land and the house next door. Tore the houses down to make a parking lot. The garage is still standing.

Memories of 353 S. Algonquin Ave.

Loved our old piano in the basement and big round table.
Spent a lot of time with our friends studying, playing games, etc. Our house was kind of a meeting place where everyone loved to come. We played cards and games at our big dining room table. Kids always wanted my Dad included when we played.

4th Of July Celebration – always had neighbors (Roth's) over for a picnic in the backyard. Dad would get his sawhorses out and

put a huge piece of plywood on top and that was our picnic table. Didn't have fancy backyard furniture like people have today. After picnic, the Dads would take us to West High School to the fireworks that were held in the stadium. What beautiful fireworks.

Things I Remember Growing Up

Diamond Milk was delivered to our house.

Mr. Peanut – (Planters Peanut) store was located on West Broad St. with a Big Mr. Peanut sign on the outside. What a great smell walking in the store. We had a cousin that when he came to town the first place he wanted to go to was to see Mr. Peanut. Then on to the Seven Wonders of the World.

Piano Lessons – my teacher was Mrs. Barbara Cable. She lived on S. Huron Ave. across from Westgate Elementary School. I would walk back and forth to lessons. I remember I practiced and practiced and then at the recital I would forget my piece. My brother never practiced and he played perfectly at the recital.

Sandy's Hamburgers was at the corner of Sullivant Ave. and Demorest Rd., where the KFC is now located.

Memories of Big Bear Store on West Broad Street

Was really the only big store on the Westside at that time. There was a S&H Green Stamps Store in the basement. We always loved to roam around basement for many things to look at.

Memories of Hilltop Record Newspaper

Was a local paper and carriers were students that delivered it once a week. Carriers collected the money for the paper once a month. I helped my brother deliver the paper.

This photo, taken in 1966 or 1967, shows the Big Bear grocery store, which was located east of Roys Avenue on West Broad Street.

PEANUT BRITTLE   *Submitted by Paul Wilson*

2 cups sugar
1 cup white Karo syrup
2 cups raw Spanish Peanuts

1 cup hot water
1 pat of butter
1 tsp baking soda

Boil sugar, syrup and water together until it spins a thread.

**Add peanuts and cook until brown
(3 to 4 minutes on high heat) stirring continually.**

Remove from heat. Add butter and soda. Stir then pour on greased cookie sheet while foaming. Use a big cookie sheet!

Little E: He Ain't Nothin' But a Hound Dog!

Submitted by Maria True

My cousin lived in Westgate for years and I had always admired her house. I loved the uniqueness of the neighborhood and the house with the original woodwork and fireplace. When she decided to sell I knew I had to have it.

After moving in I realized while the 23 windows provided much natural light, they also needed window treatments. It took awhile to dress them all but it allowed me to make the house my own.

My son, Kevin AKA "Little E" has been entertaining as an Elvis impersonator for years. He began his career at Park West and is a regular at the St. Mary Magdalene Annual Festival.

Kevin's favorite song is "Blue Suede Shoes" and loves to entertain the crowd with his Elvis moves. He has also been known to pass out plush hound dogs, Teddy bears and Hawaiian leis.

Kevin and I also love Westgate and all it has to offer.

My Four Westgate Homes

Submitted by Debbie Whitehead Maddox

Westgate has always been my home. I was born and raised here, went to Westgate Elementary school and graduated from West High. With the exception of 9 months when I lived in an apartment off Eakin Road, I have never lived anywhere else.

I lived at 42 S. Huron from 1967 to 1982. The neighbors all watched out for each other, my friends and I were able to ride bikes on the street or sidewalk without worrying about traffic, we played in the alley, had Binns Island and the Masonic Temple when we wanted to play ball and we were within a stone's throw of the library, which was located at the corner of Broad and Binns at that time.

In 1982 we moved to 2937 Fremont. That house was perfect because the large finished basement had a pool table and the garage was big enough for building West High parade floats. Our wedding reception was held in the backyard in 1988. My parents still live there and now our son and his friends use the pool table.

My husband Shawn and I purchased our first Westgate house in 1989. We moved to 351 Binns Blvd. and quickly learned how much work (and money) it takes to renovate an older home! We welcomed our son Josh to our family in 1991 and he enjoyed 5 years in this home.

In 1996 we had the wonderful opportunity to purchase my favorite home in Westgate, 3033 Palmetto St. This home came complete with neighbors who quickly became part of our family. The Clarks, Lloyd (Clarkie), Minnie and daughter Dottie, actually played a part in my life when I was a student at Westgate Elementary. My friends and I used to skip up the driveway of 3039 Palmetto and walk through the back yard of 3033 Palmetto every day to get to school. Clarkie, retired postmaster of the Hilltop Station, lived at 3039 Palmetto and met us every morning with their dog Heidi. He wished us a good morning with a song and smile.

I picture myself always living in Westgate! When it comes time to downsize I'll be happy to call another Westgate house my 5th home!

West High girls work to finish the 1984 Homecoming float at Debbie Whitehead's Fremont Street home.

Can–Can Chicken
~ CHICKEN CASSEROLE ~
Submitted by Charlotte Prior

2-4 oz cans of boned chicken

1 can chicken noodle soup (do not dilute)

1 can cream of mushroom soup (do not dilute)

1 can evaporated milk (do not dilute)

2 cups chow mein noodles

1 cup chopped celery

1. Mix together in large bowl.
2. Let stand 1 hour if possible.
3. Bake in a casserole dish at 350 for 1 hour.

Serves 8.

You may easily enlarge to serve more.

Black Bean Torta

Submitted by Patti Von Niessen

3 cups cooked black beans (2 cans)

2 zucchinis, halved lengthwise and thinly sliced

2 cups shredded cheddar cheese

1/4 cup veggie broth or red wine

1 tbsp oil

2 cups red onion, chopped

2 red or green peppers

2 garlic cloves minced

1 cup corn

1/4 tsp cayenne

1 tsp. cumin

6 ten inch flour tortillas

2 cups salsa

Preheat oven to 375 F

1 Purée beans and broth.

2 In large skillet heat oil then add onion, peppers, zucchini, and garlic.

3 Sauté until soft, about 10 minutes

4 Add corn, cumin, and cayenne and cook 2-3 minutes.

5 Oil or spray a spring form pan.

6 Place tortilla on bottom of pan and layer:
1/2 c. beans
1 c. veggies
1/3 c. cheese
1/3 c. salsa

7 Repeat 5 times ending with cheese.

8 Bake 45 minutes.

Let stand 5 minutes then release from pan.

Cut into wedges.

Parkside Road

Submitted by Sue (Donley) Emmelhainz

My parents built their home at 3121 Parkside in 1939. At that time there were only three other homes on the street and everything south of Sullivant Avenue were fields. Pheasants would wander into our yard in the fall.

During World War II, we planted a victory garden and after sharing with the neighbors we would sell any remaining corn for 15¢ a dozen.

Westgate Park looked much different in the 1940's. Before the current parking lot, there was a big hill where we all would sled in the winter. I even tried to ski, without much success.

The Hilltop Bean Dinner used to be a three-day event, complete with a carnival, rides and even a parade.

When my parents passed away my husband, Bob and I bought their home in 1975.

I enjoyed growing up in Westgate and now love living here.

BATS!

As told to Betty Jaynes by Turner Wolfenberger

We moved to Westgate in 2004. I love to tell the story about the night my sister, Raulegh, heard something in her room. My Dad thought she was just having a nightmare, but when he flipped on the light he saw his own worst nightmare ... a bat!

He opened a window and the bat disappeared ... he thought.

Later, when my grandmother came home and opened the bedroom door out flew the bat. The entire family used brooms to guide the little critter out the back door.

To this day, both my brother and I like bats ... my sister, not so much.

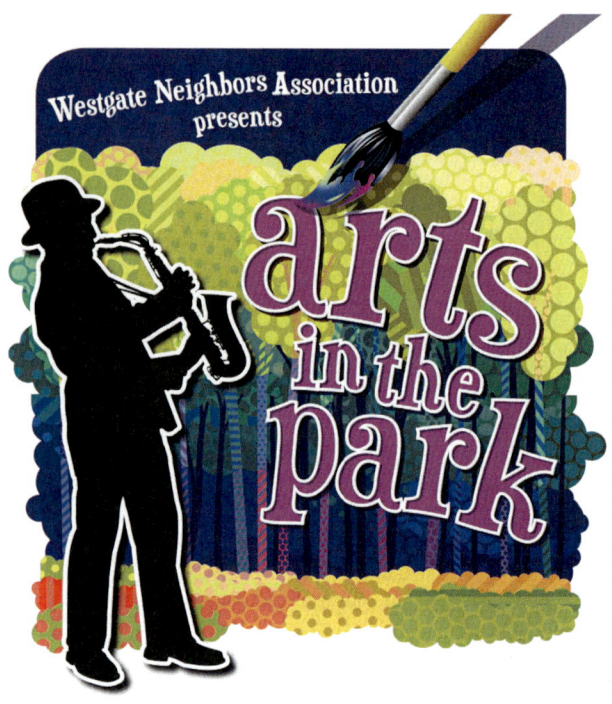

Westgate's Arts in the Park, sponsored by the WNA and supported with grants from the United Way, the Greater Columbus Arts Council and Columbus Recreation and Parks Department, was our neighborhood's contribution to the Columbus bicentennial celebration. The first-ever series of free outdoor musical performances and art exhibitions in Westgate Park featured neighborhood and area musicians and artists. The festival included activities for kids and the creation of a mural depicting 200 children playing in the park. The concept for the mural was developed by Westgate artist Aaron Grover, and all of the painting was done by artists who reside in the area.

183

ACKNOWLEDGEMENTS

It is always dangerous to single out contributors because this book is good precisely because there were many people who worked behind the scenes. The following people however contributed so greatly that they deserve special recognition. We hope all that worked on this book take pride in what they helped to produce.

Book committee members John Futty and Sue Laughlin, plus Westgate Neighbors Association (WNA) member Dick Hoffman, researched Columbus city directories, publications of the Hilltop Historical Society, *The Columbus Dispatch, The Columbus Citizen-Journal* and Franklin County auditor records for several articles. Committee member Betty Jaynes interviewed proprietors of Westgate businesses and others. Resident interviews were also conducted by committee members Sharon Muller, Shawn Maddox and Melissa Rentko. Committee members Mari Ann Futty and Debbie Maddox edited, organized and stored submitted information. Matt Hazelbaker helped with proof reading. Design and layout of the book was done by committee member Alan Jazak of Formation Studio. Thank you to pilot Jerry Ziglar and photographer Bob Smith for submitting aerial shots of Westgate.

We appreciate the cooperation of individuals associated with the Hilltop, U.S.A. Memories Facebook page and the Hilltop Historical Society for sharing photographs and historical information.

To all who agreed to be interviewed, submitted memories and/or pictures, we extend a BIG thank you. We have been delighted (and somewhat overwhelmed!) with the participation and response to this project.

Sandy Whitehead
Book Committee chair

Special Note: *Other than editing for space, the memories have been published as received, and the recipes have not been tested. The WNA is not responsible for incorrect information, grammar, or the outcome of recipes.*